Praise for *Secrets of a Fix-Up Fanatic*

"Susan Shapiro's writing is feisty and funny on the outside—
with warmth and depth on the inside—an appealing hybrid
of humor and candor."
—Karen Salmansohn,
author of *How to Be Happy, Dammit and Ballsy*

Praise for *Lighting Up*

"Shapiro's funny and nakedly honest voice is irresistible. . . .
Another great reason to lose sleep besides sex."
—Susan Jane Gilman,
author of *Hypocrite in a Pouffy White Dress*

"A mind-bendingly good read."
—*O, The Oprah Magazine*

"Frank and darkly funny."
—*New York Times Book Review*

"A great voice . . . In the end, you can't help liking her, and
waiting eagerly for the next installment of her memoirs."
—*New York Newsday*

"This fascinating memoir takes readers along Shapiro's
insightful and vulnerable journey . . . raw and relatable."
—*Cleveland Plain Dealer*

"The manic energy Shapiro brings to her life instills her
memoir with a theatrical freshness."
—*Kirkus Reviews*

"Funny . . . smart, witty . . . lightning fast."
—*Jerusalem Post*

"[An] inspirational and often hilarious portrait of a woman who boldly clears the smoke from her head once and for all."
—*Sunday Newark Star-Ledger*

Praise for *Five Men Who Broke My Heart*

"A sly, candid memoir . . . disarmingly frank . . . What is best about this memoir is Shapiro's desire to tell the whole truth about her delusions and obsessions, as well as her breakthroughs and triumphs."
—Pam Houston, *O, The Oprah Magazine*

"Playful . . . entertaining."
—*New York Times Book Review*

"Shapiro is bitingly funny and revealing."
—*USA Today*

"Susan Shapiro's promiscuously readable guilty pleasure of a memoir has a caustic, urbane feel . . . a Seinfeldian quest to settle accounts with five exes . . . a comedy of manners."
—*Elle*

"Witty, canny, ballsy."
—Salon.com

"These sharp, sassy city girls keep on coming. . . . Shapiro sets out, in witty one-liners, to describe the five men she has loved and lost. . . . More interesting than the men are Shapiro's wacky but warm parents. . . ."
—*Boston Sunday Globe*

ALSO BY SUSAN SHAPIRO

Five Men Who Broke My Heart
Lighting Up
Food for the Soul (co-editor)

SECRETS OF A
Fix-Up Fanatic:
HOW TO MEET & MARRY
YOUR MATCH

SUSAN SHAPIRO

DELTA TRADE PAPERBACKS

SECRETS OF A FIX-UP FANATIC
A Delta Trade Paperback / January 2007

Published by Bantam Dell
A Division of Random House, Inc.
New York, New York

Book design by Karin Batten

Library of Congress Cataloging in Publication Data

Shapiro, Susan.
Secrets of a fix-up fanatic : how to meet and marry your match /
Susan Shapiro.
p. cm.
ISBN: 978-0-385-34059-5
1. Man-woman relationships.   2. Mate selection.   3. Marriage.
I. Title.

HQ801 .S5217 2007   2006048477
646.7/7 22

Printed in the United States of America
Published simultaneously in Canada

www.bantamdell.com

BVG
10   9   8   7   6   5   4   3   2   1

To my mother and father,
in honor of their miraculous
fifty-two-year marriage

Author's Note

Names and identifying characteristics of some
people mentioned in this book have been
changed to protect privacy and so my close
friends and relatives will still speak to me.

Contents

SECRETS OF A
Fix-Up Fanatic

Introduction

That winter evening the stars aligned. My husband, Aaron, looked handsome as he introduced me around the holiday party for his TV/film colleagues, held at the infamous Friar's Club in midtown Manhattan. A male film director told me, "Aaron always speaks of you so lovingly." Two female sitcom producers praised the sparkling diamond on my finger. A few sketch comedy friends asked, "So, what are you working on?" When I mentioned my new project about being a fix-up fanatic, everyone seemed intrigued. Members of this crowd had wildly impressive careers on award-winning movies and television shows I was hot to hear the inside scoop on. Yet suddenly they were all dying to know the details of how I'd fixed up twelve marriages and had been matched up with my mate.

As I mingled, subtly stalking the waiters serving the shrimp and mini hot dog appetizers, word spread about my expertise and I soon became a magnet for the single guests in attendance. They came by to share their romantic stories, setups that went from bad to worse, breakup blues, and frustrating stats. At one point there were seven smart, great-looking unmarried men and women surrounding me, handing me their business cards and asking me questions, as if I possessed essential hidden wisdom and had the power to unlock the world's most potent mysteries and magic.

Okay, so in reality my spouse hated parties and what he was whispering in my ear all night was not, "I love you, gorgeous," but, "When the hell can we get out of here?" He accused me of breaking one of our major marriage vows—that I could go to any social gathering I wanted, provided he didn't have to go with me. I had argued that I couldn't exactly crash the festivities he was invited to "with guest" without him. He'd only reluctantly agreed to take me to the event under duress and guilt, because he thought he might have to cancel a trip we'd planned to California for my upcoming birthday, due to a last-minute change in his erratic work schedule.

A discreet and shy person by nature, Aaron cringed when his associates poured out the intimacies of their depressing dates and divorces to me right in front of him, in public. He still hadn't recovered from the time I'd relayed the remarks my protégée, Pam, had made about his buddy Carl's private parts, after their first sleepover date.

"What are you so upset about?" I'd asked. "She gave him a rave review."

"Oh God," he moaned. "Now I'll never be able to get the picture of a naked, well-endowed Carl out of my head. Will you please stay away from my friends?"

Nevertheless, it was a fun, fabulous fete, and I was proud to be on the arm of my cranky, antisocial, workaholic other half. It wasn't always this way . . .

• • • •

"So when are you getting married already? You're not getting any younger," my uncle Bruce bellowed when he saw me at his youngest son's winter wedding. Who got married in December, anyway? As if spending the holidays alone wasn't depressing enough, I couldn't look good in freezing weather when my dress was all staticky and hats and scarves made my hair frizz. But there I self-consciously was, in my midthirties, the oldest person at the singles table, pretending to be joyously celebrating the nuptials of a cousin fourteen years my junior. Once again, I was dateless and heartbroken, having just been unceremoniously dumped by yet another long-term boyfriend for unfair reasons I did not even understand. Worse, I had to be related to this insensitive moron who was loudly calling attention to my unattached status.

Sometimes singing solo in a world filled with duets totally sucked. I used to wonder what was wrong with me, fearing I'd wind up lonely forever, or settling for a partner I didn't adore—just to avoid dying alone. So I understand the anger, anxiety, and annoyance that's caused my unwed pals to tell their meddling parents, "Enough already! You're not getting any grandkids from me. Go buy a puppy." I get why it's easier to stay home wearing sweats, eating chocolate chip ice cream from the pint, and watching reruns of *Sex and the City*, giving up on the whole mess of mixing, mating, and matrimony.

I felt that way too. I had no idea that finding love could be so natural, easy, and comforting. But then I discovered the trick move that transformed everything: I asked for help from a few close friends. Yes, instead of speed dating, barhopping, text messaging former lovers for late-night booty calls, or cruising cyberspace for airbrushed pictures of deceptive strangers across the country, I did something so retro it was revolutionary. I actually inquired if two nice human beings in my life, whom I knew well and trusted, would fix me up. These two sympathetic souls became my love mentors. They led me directly to my smart, witty, and wonderful spouse, spun me around every time I almost screwed up the relationship, and then danced at my wedding.

I bet that you too are already connected to important, kind, cool people who care about you and your future. Chances are they're staring you in the face every day and, quite frankly, they're getting tired of hearing you kvetch that all the good ones are taken, complain that online daters keep lying to you about their age, looks, salary, and marital status, and list all the new reasons you have to hate your psycho ex. You call these patient listeners your workmates, classmates, teammates, and roommates. (Notice they have the word *mate* in their names!) There's also your best pals, understanding bosses, regular clients, favorite teachers, friendly neighbors, and caring family members. (After you weed through the insensitive monsters, most clans have a few sweet cousins, siblings, aunts, or uncles who'll be on your side.) You don't realize it yet, but one of these nurturing individuals, whom you already like, see, and socialize with, is the ideal matchmaker to set you up with your match.

I know this because as a fix-up fanatic, I've set up most of my single relatives, cohorts, and colleagues. Aside from the dozen marriages under my belt, I have two current cohabitations, seven serious liaisons lurking, and a few flings still flinging. One well-wisher insists I now have a condominium complex reserved for me in heaven. My couples have so far produced fifteen offspring, including four Michigan munchkins who belong to my brother Brian and his wife, Monica, my former coworker and confidante. So perhaps, like the fertility doctor in Milan Kundera's novel *The Farewell Party*, who secretly injects childless women with his own sperm, I have been diabolically trying to exert my influence over the universe. Or at least, thanks to my brother's four adorable kids, I have found a roundabout way to quiet my folks' requests for grandchildren.

My preoccupation with the passion of others is partially payback to the cosmic wedding gods. I owe them big ever since Valerie, my former boss, set me up with Aaron, the sardonic TV/film writer who, for the last decade, I have been very happy to call my husband. Before I coerced a reluctant Aaron to pledge "I do," Emma, a kind women's-magazine editor I freelanced for, fixed me up with Joshua. He was a charming psychoanalyst who made the procrastinating, commitment-phobic Aaron jealous enough to propose. Upon hearing my newly engaged status, Joshua sweetly asked, "Can I be your second husband?" Joshua has since married too, and we have remained each other's fans and e-mail allies, with no need for seconds on anything.

That connection came full circle when Emma and I recently cohosted a press reception for Joshua's new nonfiction book. There Emma's older brother Barry, a professor who happened to be Joshua's best friend, clicked with Cara, my architect crony. Barry and Cara went from looking like tired, middle-aged divorcés to starry-eyed sweethearts in what seemed like seconds. "I waited forty-nine years to meet the love of my life," Barry recently shared.

Are you getting the picture of how to find that special someone yet? Hint: turn off your computer, fax, iPod, Game Boy, cell phone, and BlackBerry, and invite your friends and siblings over.

Trying to meet somebody on my own in the big city for fifteen years before I wed, at age thirty-five, was rough. It involved fits, starts, and losing at love so often that certain oafs in my inner circle expressed their sexist opinion that I would be an "old maid" or "spinster" forever (while single older men were annoyingly referred to as "eligible bachelors" and "good catches"). Still, my humiliating breakups were good for something—they provided lots of raw material to bring to the weekly writing workshop I held at my apartment. While we ate popcorn and critiqued each other's lines of lust and longing, some of my fellow scribes were more into flirting than fixing stanzas. Three couples wound up combining quicker than you could craft couplets in iambic pentameter. Along with food and wine to feed the group, I subsequently had to purchase a trio of wedding presents—and three baby gifts.

Luckily, my loveless exploits led to a book where I chronicled going back to revisit the biggest heartbreaks from my past. Performing exit interviews with five former boyfriends I'd deemed immature, unready, and unfaithful, I ended up pinpointing the moment where I myself had screwed up each long-term liaison! This taught me that it took two not to tango, and that there were three sides to every story: his, hers, and the right one. Although it's easier to blame someone else than to examine your own failures, I learned that challenging and questioning yourself gets you much farther than playing victim. Then I set up my book editor Dina with Ted, a comedy protégé of Aaron's. I got a second book out of the deal; she got a good-humored husband.

So unlike all those "relationship experts" out there who are incapable of having a real relationship, or who married in their twenties, and then again in their thirties, and maybe even had a third go-round in their forties, I have witnessed—and scored—on all sides of the setup spectrum. I have learned how to charm a blind date or two, end an almost ideal match with amity, close the deal with my personal Mr. Perfect, keep my first (and I hope only) union rapturous, and expertly hook up other sets.

I've also regularly shared my sharp-tongued, politically

incorrect, provocative, and sometimes downright subver-sive suggestions on every stage of dating and domestic rela-tions. This has led to more than one confidante screaming, "What, are you insane? That is simply ridiculous! Nobody ever told me that before," then showing up three weeks later with flowers, whispering, "Thanks, our sex life has never been better."

Aaron abhors when I steal all of his single confreres for fodder. Nor does he like it when I'm preoccupied and busy, offering others free cyberadvice at all hours of the day and night. He fears that my sideline is a borderline erotic obses-sion, worried it reveals that some part of me still wants to be out there and available. It's the exact opposite, I con-stantly argue. I'm a die-hard romantic optimist who feels so lucky to have him that it compels me to keep connecting other couples. Aaron, a cynical misanthrope who thinks we marry our dark side, insists there must be more sinister mo-tives lurking. Okay, so maybe I am a control freak who digs the perks of pairing people off. In my social milieu, when you fix up a duo that winds up dancing down the aisle, you are showered with flowers, invitations, lovely gifts, and gratitude, and become part of the legacy passed down from children to grandchildren. Matchmaking makes me feel special—the center of all mystical forces, the love guru.

It has been suggested that I start my own business and be-come a professional marriage broker. Yet I have no interest whatsoever in joining any Romeos and Juliets for financial remuneration. I have turned down multiple offers for cash, cars, and apartments on Fifth Avenue. I said no to my pal Lloyd, a Long Island plastic surgeon, when he offered any free cosmetic procedure I wanted if I located a mate for Ivy, his forty-year-old sister. He was even willing to throw in a touch-up for every child produced by the potential union. While hosting a singles-only dinner, I introduced Ivy to

Rich, who became her groom and the father of her baby son. Yet the desire to be the go-between was stirred by sincere sentiment for Ivy. Also, Ivy and Lloyd's mother, Selma, and my mother, Miriam, were best buddies growing up on the Lower East Side of New York. So introducing Ivy to her other half had nothing to do with free goods or liposuction (tempting though it was), and more to do with the aura of fate and ancient family lore.

Promoting legal partnership for people I care about feels natural and fun. After all, being in a strong marriage is the healthiest, safest, most joyous way to exist. Staying hitched even gives you a wedlock bonus, increasing your life expectancy by as much as nine years, according to the National Center for Health Statistics. Betting there's a fix-up boon too, I'm convinced that the more loving couples I help create, the longer my own connubial and career bliss will continue. As my mother's proverb goes, "A good deed always returns to you—but not if that's the reason you do it." When you've been lucky enough to get everything you've wanted from the world, you have to give back to keep up the good karma.

I'll never forget my own misconceptions about who was marriage material and how they were corrected. Right after my wise, wonderful fixer-upper Valerie set me up with Aaron, I'd stopped by to thank her but said, "He's very smart and sweet, but I don't think he's my type." Valerie, who was ten years my senior and happily wed herself, smiled and patted my head. Then she yelled in my face, "Don't be insane! Your last two boyfriends were selfish morons who screwed around on you! Aaron is gorgeous, brilliant, and a good, honest person who could actually take care of you. He's not your type? Are you crazy? If you have half a brain, you'll marry this one before someone smarter steals him from right under you!"

That's what's so great about finding the right match-maker. Sycophants are useless. You need a romantic guidance counselor who will candidly clue you in if you're doing something wrong and show you how to amend your attitude to get what you want. In my case, being open to Valerie's point of view led me to a ring, real romance, and (so far) a decade of domestic harmony that I didn't believe could ever happen to me.

I bet you're beginning to think that true love isn't in the stars for you, and that your single status might somehow involve eternal bad luck, loner DNA, or destiny. But forget the metaphysics and metaphors and face facts. If you've tried to find a partner on your own for years and have not succeeded, do something different! You just need a little help and a fresh perspective. So give up complete control and let go of the close-minded opinion that only you can possibly know what's going to be good for you in the future. Instead, put your heart in the hands of an honest, caring, outspoken, strong-minded setter-upper. This will be especially useful if, like me, you have a tendency to be strong, independent, pigheaded, self-sufficient, and a tiny bit afraid of what you deserve and desire most: true intimacy.

1

THE ARGUMENT FOR POSTMODERN MATCHMAKING

There are many different methods for making love connections and I offer no value judgments—except to say that being fixed up by someone you know is the best way to meet your mate. Having a comrade, coworker, or cousin you love set you up for free is the oldest, cheapest, fastest, safest, and nicest route to landing a different kind of love. You get to bypass the usual complex weeding-out process and sidestep the awkward ways that singles usually intersect. These are often so uncomfortable and agonizing that there's a cottage industry of magazine articles, books, sitcoms, movies, and reality shows chronicling the annals of disastrous dates. By choosing and using a matchmaker you know, you can:

- Avoid bars, concerts, raves, clubs, and other meat markets—the most obvious places to connect with drunks and creeps who could be trying to seduce, drug, manipulate, rob, molest, date-rape, or take advantage of you.

- Never again have to approach a stranger of the opposite sex whom you've never met with a pickup line (like "Come here often?") or silly ploy (like "Can you tell me what time it is?"). Instead, the person you meet for coffee has already agreed in advance to give you a shot. Your date knows all about you; you know all about your date. You have an intrusive matchmaker in common to comfortably gossip about, which will break the ice.

- Steer clear of the Internet, which can sometimes offer the quickest, most impatient path to unwittingly picking up pedophiles, ex-cons, losers, and liars from different states and countries who post ten-year-old pictures of themselves with all kinds of other deceptive misinformation.

- Remember how liberating it feels to detach from your laptop, cell phone, video games, TiVo, and all your other high-tech gadgets, take a shower, and get dressed up to socialize with warm people you already like and whomever they choose for your ready-made date.

- Save yourself the agony of placing personal ads, the easiest approach to becoming a confused and insecure liar yourself. Has anyone in history ever offered a résumé or recent photograph that honestly reflects true appearance, age, height, weight, profession, salary, original hair color, or reason for past breakups?

- Give up trying to brand, market, sell, package, and repackage yourself—as if you were a product like cream cheese, or a movie that could be summed up in cute sound bites (rather than a whole, complicated, interesting, real person worthy of an entire conversation).

- Stop wasting your time and throwing away your hard-earned cash on expensive matchmaking services, the clearest gateway to lose your savings to businessmen and women (who are usually miserably single) to do the superficial sorting for you. I only recommend amateur setter-uppers like me, where no money changes hands.

- Skip attending all generic singles events you have to pay for that are given by fly-by-night organizations you've never heard of before. Thus you can cease the painful practice that erodes the confidence, spunk, and great energy you'll need to connect with nice, normal, fun suitors in your own social realm.

Many people still harbor old-fashioned and negative notions of matchmaking. But nobody is suggesting that you allow family members to force you down the aisle with somebody of your faith, ethnic background, or social strata, for purposes of parent pleasing, political diplomacy, or procreation. I'm a huge advocate of staying single for as long as that makes you happy, and dating around until you feel good and ready to settle down. I'm also a champion of feminism, gay rights, and every kind of mixed marriage there is—as long as your mate mixes in love and kindness. Being fixed up by someone you know, trust, and have picked yourself creates a totally different aura than the menacing mood of *Fiddler on the Roof*'s Yenta. In the postmodern matchmaking arena, you are always in total control of your dates and your destiny. You get to say yes or no to potential get-togethers on a day-to-day basis. (Though please note that answering "Okay, I'll give it a shot," will lead you to "I do" much faster than saying, "I have a zit in the middle of my face, so I can't meet someone new tonight," "I need to watch the basketball game," or "I'm not going out in the rain now 'cause it'll frizz my hair.")

If there is nobody in your life whom you know, like, and trust enough to let set you up, we may have just pinpointed exactly what's been stopping you from finding the right partner. Future chapters will help you combat social isolation and teach you how to cultivate a crowd to care about and connect you. More often the issue is that you're too embarrassed to admit you're feeling sad, stuck, or lonely when it comes to the love department. I'll also discuss in detail the best, fastest, and least painful ways to ask for and get a little romantic assistance.

The beauty of having someone near and dear set you up is that there'll be no surprises or shocks about what lies ahead. You probably already know your matchmakers' marital status, their mates, and whether you trust their stance on sexual matters and methods of socializing. Thus you can feel semicertain that your next suitor will not be a tranny in hiding, a serial adulterer, or an axe murderer. You can also easily find out what your match's ex looked like and learn all kinds of other important data about your date before you even sit down for drinks or a casual lunch at your local diner. I've been known to let slip whether a client is currently looking for fun for the next few years or matrimony within six months; if either side comes with a car, a country house, or a dog or cat or canary; and whether someone is desperate to have offspring tomorrow or is anti-children. Serial monogamists who have a history of never being able to close the deal come with a warning label.

Furthermore, a fair fixer-upper will not mince words when it comes to mismatches, misgivings, or misogyny. My sweet former student Sasha came to a recent party I threw, but ignored the earnest gentlemen I introduced her to. Instead she gravitated toward an alluring teacher I knew to have a reputation as a roué. When Sasha informed me of his interest, I told her plainly: "Fine, go out and have a drink with him, if you must. But do not sleep with him. Ever. For any reason." Sasha went out to dinner with him twice before he became verbally abusive. She stopped by last week to thank me for the advance advisory. Luckily, most matchmakers have wide word-of-mouth networks, an effective technique that perhaps inspired all the bad-date whistle-blowing blogs and dot-coms that have recently become so popular.

George, a thirty-seven-year-old friend of a friend, contacted me about a month ago. He said he was single and quite eager to go out with Julie, a pretty, well-known thirty-seven-year-old celebrity acquaintance of mine he had a crunch on. He thought that since we knew someone in common, I would quickly provide the intro, or just hand him Julie's private e-mail address and phone number. Not so fast, buster! First I had a few questions for him. After a blunt back-and-forth online tête-à-tête, I gathered that George already had a spouse whom he had left—and not very long ago. When I pressed for more details, he reluctantly admitted that they weren't yet divorced, nor even legally separated. I promptly deleted him from Julie's current date card. If he managed to meet her himself, that was his business. But I would not be the liaison. Had he been straightforward from the start about his status, I might have found him more on the up-and-up. Yet when I was living solo, I wouldn't be in such a rush to rendezvous with a man three minutes after he ruined his marriage.

"How do you know it was the husband's fault?" Aaron wanted to know. "What if it was the wife who screwed up the marriage?"

"A guy who has just been dumped would not be feeling confident enough to make a play for a beautiful, famous woman," I told him. "Plus, people who've been screwed over usually play the sympathy card by saying, 'My wife just left me.'"

"What if it was a mutual decision to break up?" Aaron continued to defend all of mankind.

I considered Aaron's defense of this male he had never even met and conceded it was possible. But even if the demise of George's domestic scenario wasn't at all his fault, he had legal entanglements to take care of before he was ready for the kind of full-speed-ahead fix-up Julie said she wanted. Since she was thirty-seven and had never been married, she was focused on finding a mate and having a baby right away. Thus I didn't want Julie to waste time, money, or energy on someone not as ready or as forthright as she was, not to mention that he was still literally wed to somebody else he owned a home with.

Sorry if I sound prudish, but I figured from experience that if George couldn't be totally straight with me—a potentially ideal love connector—he could lie or withhold important information from his dates too, perhaps until after they were postcoital. As a married woman who'd been around the block with bad boyfriends, and had learned how to weed through a lot of weasels to find my own rare and honorable hero, I wasn't playing games here. I was more like the referee calling out-of-bounds.

Still, I wasn't sending George to the penalty box to punish him for real or imagined transgressions. I was basically just implying, "Come back when you are officially available," and filed his request in the back of my mind to revisit at a later date, after his divorce papers were filed. I knew somebody who knew George's soon-to-be-ex-wife, and made a mental note to see if I could get her side of the story. Amazing what a matchmaker's fact-finding mission sometimes revealed.

So what if George wound up frustrated or annoyed? I didn't want to court any headaches, and was only in the market for real husband material for my clients. It didn't matter to me if I won or lost a popularity contest among cads not up to the high standards of my romantic roster. If he turned out to be a decent fellow as a divorcé, I could always call him back to invite him to a singles soiree. If he didn't come, who cared? How refreshing not to give a damn if he didn't like me.

The point is that these kind of in-depth, behind-the-scenes interactions are another huge perk of having someone you know matchmaking for you. Since we know who we are setting up personally, we take everything very personal. We have a shared goal, and our reputation as a perceptive, smart, and serious fixer-upper is at stake. One misstep could hurt someone we care about, along with our future prospects. So we apply protective filters and shields, assessing each member of the potential gene pool so you don't have to second-guess who is not earnest, for real, worthy, or good enough for you. We offer you a divine yin-yang balance to unburden you and keep you sane and serene. We can be a pest, or a pain, or a flaming bitch so you don't have to be. You can remain shy, retiring, passive, forgiving, and/or flirtatious while we do the sorting, heavy lifting, research, dirty work, and rejecting.

Yes, there are cynics out there who think a fixer-upper procures partners like a pimp. In actuality, a good matchmaker is part older sibling, part private detective, part shrink, part bully, and part volunteer bodyguard out there to protect you.

If you're the least bit nervous about trying the matchmaker method, ask yourself one question. Who do you trust more—your sister, boss, and best friend? Or out-of-town companies wanting to make big bucks on your loneliness by linking you to their cyberclients around the country, with no legal motive or ability to check any facts or verify anybody's posted vital statistics?

Indeed, when *The New York Times* "Modern Love" column editor Daniel Jones was asked to share his observations about trends in twenty-first-century dating, he deduced that, "In pursuing love, electronic communication allows us to be more reckless, fake, distracted and isolated than ever before." Jones, the editor of the popular male essay anthology *The Bastard on the Couch*, opined that "men and women today are apt to plunge into love affairs via text message, cut them off by PowerPoint, lie about who they are and what they want in forums and blogs and online dating sites, pretend they're young when they're old and old when they're young, ignore the people they're physically with for those who are a keystroke away, shoo their children off their laps to caress their BlackBerrys, and spend untold hours staring at pixilated porn stars."

So when you're finished playing with cyberfire, failing, and paying for services that often disappoint you, then come back down to earth, where your fellow earthlings can lead you to lasting love cost-free. If you're still skeptical, examine the motives of people you know to set you up. Members of your family want you to go forth and multiply your tribe, which is their tribe. Most friends and colleagues who are amateur setter-uppers want to help you out of the goodness of their heart, a much sweeter motive than profit. Those who are married hope you join their ranks of those bound in holy matrimony, which reinforces their own choices. Single fix-up fanatics, like Alicia Silverstone's character on the recent TV series *Miss Match*, often unconsciously feel that by giving you love they will find love themselves. What's not to love about that?

Plus, all matchmakers relish sharing their own romantic lessons and following up on their pet projects. You know who they are, where they are coming from, and you can hear examples and swap stories often, over the phone and in the flesh. So you will be able to endlessly discuss and dissect the interesting two-hour date you just went on, with the one person on the planet who is almost as emotionally invested in the final outcome as you are.

Furthermore, cultivating a few matchmakers from your inner circle will force you to get out of your house, your head, and your cybersystem. You will have to get over your shyness, timidity, doubts, hesitations, fears, insecurities, shame, and seclusion. You'll need to take some chances, make decisions, and ask someone you know for exactly what you need—face-to-face, using direct eye contact, putting yourself on the line, and feeling very open and vulnerable. You will need to ask questions, answer them, argue, risk rejection, and otherwise intimately relate to a living, breathing being who cares about you. This important exercise in continual complex social interaction will provide excellent practice for dealing with the living, breathing mate with whom you will soon be spending your future.

2

HOW TO FIX UP YOURSELF FIRST

Do you want to hang out with a screwed-up, depressed, un-employed, broke, insecure, out-of-touch, self-involved, needy mess? No? Guess what? Nobody else does either. The best way to get a good mate is to get yourself together so you can be a good mate.

Fifteen years ago, when I was complaining that my then-boyfriend, Aaron, was not making me happy, my former therapist, Dr. Patricia Gross, stopped me cold when she said: "Love doesn't make you happy; make yourself happy." That turned out to be the most helpful, illuminating advice about relationships that I ever received.

Not only were those eight simple words completely on target, but they basically explained to me what had been amiss with all of my former boyfriends. I had scrutinized, analyzed, and blamed each one of them for being selfish, unfair, imperfect, superficial, vain, and/or not ready to commit. It was so much easier to find fault with them than to look inside and acknowledge my own failures and limitations. My biggest block was that I had lingered under the universal yet unhealthy illusion that having the right person by my side would be enough to heal my deep wounds, imperfections, and everything else wrong with me. Thus I was looking to my lover to take care of, please, and entertain me too much, sidestepping the important work I needed to do on myself. I had so overburdened partners from my past that my previous relationships imploded from the weight of my unrealistic expectations.

Are you doing the same thing? Here's how to tell. When you wonder why your old affairs didn't last, do you mostly focus on how your partner didn't make you happy and wasn't really there for you? If so, you need to refocus, asking new, better, and smarter questions. Why weren't you making yourself happy? Why weren't *you* there for you? Whether your former mate was a good or a bad person isn't really the issue. Yes, your old lovers might have been immature, idiotic, or inadequate. But it's not your job to analyze, criticize, or fix them after the fact. It's your job to understand how and why your own low self-esteem or lack of insight led you to allow someone unworthy of your love into your bed and your head. It's also your job to determine if this was a decent shot that just didn't work out, a one-time mistake, or part of a larger pattern and problem.

Petra, a divorced restaurant manager who wanted me to fix her up, argued that sometimes in a breakup only one person deserves the blame. Petra was sure that was the case with her and her ex-husband of twenty years, an engineer who was an abusive alcoholic. She never drank, she was never mean or abusive, and she'd desperately wanted the union to work out. Thus she insisted that the twenty wasted years of their union was all his fault.

"When you met, how long did it take you to figure out he was a problem drinker?" I asked.

"I knew within the first year," she admitted.

"So forget about him. Let's talk about why you stayed for the next nineteen years," I said.

Now, *that* was a fascinating conversation. It turned out that Petra's father had been an alcoholic, and her mother had eventually helped him get sober. Petra had it in her head that she had to play the role of her husband's caretaker, sponsor, and saint, and thus be just like her long-suffering mother. Yet Petra said she didn't want her mother's life, and acknowledged that she would have been better off divorcing years sooner. Now that she was free and dating again in her forties, Petra confided that this first guy she'd sparked with—a coworker she'd gone out with a few times—turned out to have a gambling problem. Instead of running the other way, she thought she could help him quit. This didn't surprise me. We all have inherent patterns, usually stemming from our upbringing, that we have to struggle with and unravel. Until Petra could iron out her own emotional confusions and injuries, I bet that she wouldn't even be able to feel attracted to somebody not addicted and healthy.

There is only one person on the planet who can cure you, conquer your conflicts, fully protect you, and make your life fantastic and fulfilling: you. Here is the best rule I have ever heard for romance: the happier, better, and stronger you are by yourself, the happier, better, and stronger the connections you will create. Despite all the cute Hallmark cards and sappy song lyrics, nobody else can finish you, complete you, make you whole, make your life complete, be your everything, or make your life worth living. You have to learn to be whole and complete all by your lonesome before you will be able to bond well with another human being. In fact, this equation is essential before, during, and after you wed. It might even be the determining factor whether you end up living happily ever after or bitterly divorced and alone.

Alissa, a Los Angeles journalist I know, recently called me to complain that her lawyer husband, Joe, wasn't really making enough money to support her and their three kids the way she wanted. He was spending too much on his fishing and boating hobbies, money she felt should be spent on her and their family. Furthermore, he was selfishly planning a weekend trip to Chicago with his old college buddies, without her. I liked Joe and from what I could tell, he was a faithful, hardworking husband and terrific father. He respected Alissa's career and never complained when she took business trips. Plus, she wanted lots of kids, and though Joe thought three was enough, Alissa had been pushing for a fourth child. He didn't say no; he was currently considering it. In lieu of commiserating with Alissa and suggesting ways she should redo her spouse and his finances, I turned the tables on her and examined what was going awry in *her* life, habits, work, and head.

"If your career were taking off, and *you* were on your way to Chicago to promote your hot new book on *Oprah*, how would you feel?" I asked. Alissa admitted she'd be thrilled and excited. On deeper inquiry, she confessed that she'd then have no problem with Joe's activities. Indeed, she'd be relieved that he had his own interests and passions so she could keep pursuing her dream. Plus she always felt better traveling when she knew he'd be with the kids every night.

Instead of constantly harping on what he wasn't doing for her, I advised Alissa to try complimenting Joe on the good things he was doing: working hard, remaining a faithful husband, being a good dad—the list was vast. She also needed to uncover exactly why she couldn't finish the book she wanted to write, make more money with her work, and provide for herself. I suggested she reexamine her priorities. Everything comes at a cost, and you can't just blindly assume that you can have every single thing you want in the world when you want it. If taking care of her children was getting in the way of her heart's biggest desire, and that was to publish her book, why did she want another baby so soon? Was trying to get everything at the same time a way to sabotage herself and her success? I suggested she compromise her rigid schedule and time frame, reexamine her expectations, and stop assuming her husband's task was to satisfy—and pay for—her every whim. That was her own task. Rather than resent Joe's few forays into making himself happy, she needed to give him space to find himself, be himself, connect with his friends, and reenergize. Two people who are strong separately will be stronger together.

At first she was offended by my harsh assessment. But then Alissa e-mailed a month later to say she'd encouraged Joe to take his trip. He'd come back feeling relaxed and filled with buoyant stories about his friends that made him seem more adventurous and attractive. She'd also started a new writing group she loved, which made her feel more inspired to finish her book project on a day-to-day basis. And yes, she added, her sex life with her husband was spicier too.

It's much easier to blame our discontent and angst on our mate, rather than solve our own confusions and crises. Yet even if it appears as though someone else's love can fill, fulfill, or save you, it rarely works out in the long term. Several years ago I read an interview with a beautiful, well-known actress who said that even though she knew you were supposed to love yourself first before falling in love, she did it the other way around. She fell in love with herself through her famous husband falling for her. At the time I remember thinking Oh no! Don't do it that way! It doesn't work! Do it the other way! She was rich, successful, thin, witty, and gorgeous. But that was not enough to trick the truth and skip the self-esteem step. When she and her husband broke up, it didn't shock me. You really have to first learn to love and accept yourself completely before you can eternally bond with another human being. This is not something you can get out of, like gym class, a social obligation, or jury duty. If you try to work around it, it will come back to haunt you later.

I can't tell you how many single men and women I've met who, after asking to be fixed up, have confessed to me that deep down they feel like a lonely, confused, unworthy, self-destructive mess. They are without a career they care about, don't have a comfortable place to call home, lack special friends, are not in touch with any family members who enhance their world, and don't take good care of themselves. They admit that they don't have a game plan—except to find somebody to support them, heal them, and make their world better. I realize that many people want to rush into romance right after a life-changing transition such as a death, divorce, breakup, firing, eviction, graduation, or a big move across country. And I know that people going through major changes can have extreme mood swings. Yet I will not even attempt to set up someone who is in a negative, sad, self-destructive, twisted, or troubled state of mind. Experience has proven to me that someone in an ugly, messy mood will create an ugly, messy entanglement, and I do not want anything to do with that.

I will, however, happily hand over an e-mail address where he or she can apply for a potential internship, an interesting class or seminar, a new job, a flier for a fun upcoming reading, info on a better sublet, the location of an art, theater, or writing workshop, a local AA group, or the phone number of a good nearby therapist. Vulnerability can be endearing, and if someone tells me she's lonely, I have been known to invite her to my next party right on the spot. Often the difference between a loser going nowhere and someone capable of soon finding love is four words: Can you help me?

Of course, nobody is perfect, and sometimes the one trait missing from an otherwise fantastic person's universe really is just the right partner. Plus, one recovering from a trauma or transforming experience can feel different insecurities or fears hourly. But before you approach potential matchmakers to hook you up with available dates, you first have to ask yourself if your head and heart are in the right place for a healthy relationship right now. Have you done the hard work of learning who you are and what you need to be happy? If you have the fantasy that finding a lover is going to fix you, you'll wind up disappointed. Love will not create a life for you, it can only enhance the life you've built for yourself.

How do you tell if you're strong, kind of cranky, but basically ready to connect, or whether you need two years on the couch and a prescription for Zoloft before you sleep with anybody else?

Buy a new notebook reserved for this romantic journey you're about to embark on. Don't just answer yes or no to the following questions about the main spheres of your emotional setup. Make specific comments about what you've got covered and where improvements are needed. Instead of keeping frustrations and failures vague and hidden, taking notes and writing about where you are in life can make big, complicated, amorphous feelings more real and specific. It'll jump-start your plan for action.

Take the Ready-for-True-Romance Test

1. Do you reside in a nice house or apartment building? Is there enough space for two people to live there? Do you sleep in a comfortable bed? Is there room for someone to comfortably sleep beside you? If your stu-

dio or one-bedroom pad is on the modest or small side, but it's clean and you could make room for a companion, the answer is yes. Write "living space" and after it put a star. But if you're thirty-four and crashing indefinitely at your parents' home or tossing and turning on a broken futon every night amid a pigsty you share with four annoying roommates, you've got issues to deal with. Write a list of everything wrong with your living space and why you couldn't bring a lover home. If you can list more than ten obstacles right off the top of your head, finding a new place to live (and not a new lover) should be your priority.

Yes, there's a chance you'll meet someone with a big house and move in, or eventually buy a place together. But like the characters in Tama Janowitz's amusing insightful novel *Slaves of New York*, you never want to be stuck in a romantic situation that exists solely for the real estate. Needing a roof over your head is never a good foundation for love, especially because if the love ends, you could find yourself out on the street.

2. Are you content with the direction of your work and financial situation? If you're trying to make it as a singer/songwriter but are currently debt-free and paying your own rent as a bartender, write about all the progress you've been making. If you're a lawyer and hate it with no plans for an alternative, that's no. If you're thirty-four and have $100,000 in unpaid credit card bills, cut up your Visa and American Express cards today and buy Suze Orman's latest book—with cash. Or better yet, borrow it from the library. If you're in debt and stuck in a career rut, who would want to be stuck in that professional pit with you? The only thing more boring and depressing than hearing someone

complain about how much he hates his job, his company, or his boss, is listening to someone's excuses for why he can't find any work at all. And being around someone hiding from his creditors feels downright sleazy. Conversely, there's nothing more invigorating than spending time with someone who adores what she does. If you're going somewhere interesting, you're much more likely to find company on your journey.

3. Do you have family connections that add love or comfort to your universe? If you have normal petty fights with your parents, siblings, children, aunts, or uncles during the holidays every year, and then make up, you can answer yes. If you have not spoken to your mother, father, grandparent, sister, brother, or child for more than one year and you are not currently in some kind of counseling, answer no. Write a list of every member of your clan whom you have avoided for more than six months. Unless these exiled relatives are violent, psychotic, addicted to drugs or alcohol and refusing to get clean, or in jail, consider calling a therapist, clergy member, or other mediator to help you. I'm not implying that you are wrong about the impulse to avoid those who you know will drain you with their abusive words or toxic energy. There are ways to minimize your contact with those related to you who have annoyed or disrespected you, and often that's a good, self-protecting instinct. Personally, I prefer connecting to certain difficult relatives by phone, fax, e-mail, and snail mail, which I find less invasive and hurtful to me than huge holiday gatherings.

Yet people who cannot forgive slights—and instead blow off loved ones forever—could be extremist, escapist, fragile, intolerant, uncompromising, and/or unaccepting of their pasts. Completely slamming the door on an important relationship is not usually a good method of coping with emotional hardship and should only be used as a last resort. Trying to be tolerant and find a compromise is not a favor you do for someone else, but a gift you give yourself. What if the parent or sibling you've cut all contact with dies? Then you are stuck with unresolved guilt, which can complicate grief and threaten your peace of mind. Often someone who can walk away from an old family tie will have trouble walking into—and remaining in—a new one.

4. Are you living where you want to be geographically? If you can only afford to live in a small house in Beruyn or Blue Island, Illinois, but you're working toward being able to afford a penthouse on the Magnificent Mile in Chicago, you can answer yes, especially if you can list steps you are taking to realize your dream (like saving money, reading the real estate ads, and considering alternatives like getting a roommate). If you've always hoped to one day get out of the hellhole you're stuck in, with no plan or end in sight, write no. Can you write down everything you hate about your location and what's stopping you from leaving? What are you afraid of? Often realistic issues mirror metaphoric ones. So figuring out how to get unstuck from an unsatisfying state could also liberate you emotionally.

5. Do you have friends and colleagues you socialize with on a regular basis? If you do, even if you don't have enough time to get together more than once a week, answer yes and write down everyone you consider a

friend, an ally, or a close acquaintance. If you don't have at least five people on this list, you have to figure out why. This issue is very significant and worth solving before you look for a partner. Someone who can't make or sustain friendships usually can't make or sustain a marriage. Even if you meet your mate and are able to tie the knot, it's not good if your spouse is the only person you trust or feel close to. That much pressure and dependency could sink any relationship.

6. Do you have educational/intellectual/cultural stimulation in your day-to-day schedule? Write down twelve recent books, plays, movies, dance recitals, concerts, museums, or lectures you've enjoyed in the last year. (Video games, TV sitcoms, instant messaging, pornography, and shopping do not count as cultural stimulation.) Have you always regretted that you never finished high school, college, vocational school, or your graduate degree? Write down what you would have done differently. Then ask yourself what the hell you're waiting for.

7. Are you conquering your bad habits? Write down all of your addictions and vices. Emulate the charming, kooky heroine of *Bridget Jones's Diary* and be specific about how much you're smoking, drinking, and overeating. Being imperfect and human is perfectly acceptable. Using drugs, alcohol, cigarettes, junk food, gambling, pornography, or excessive shopping to soothe yourself and avoid facing difficult feelings on a daily basis isn't so hot. You don't realize it, but your negative compulsions could be what's getting in the way of meeting or meshing with a mate. I learned the hard way that addicts are dependent on substances, not people. It wasn't until I quit smoking, toking, and drinking that my marriage started thriving. I first had to literally get the smoke out of my eyes.

8. Do you have good health and a decent body image? Write down all the things you like about yourself. In an adjacent column, list what you don't like about yourself. Wanting to lose ten pounds and get in better shape over the next twelve months is such a common New Year's resolution that it's cliché. But being anorexic, bulimic, obese, ill without taking care of your condition, into cutting or otherwise hurting yourself, hating your body, obsessing over your imperfections, or feeling afraid to be naked with the lights on are all significant blockades. Fears and negative feelings could keep you from getting what you want and need. If the list of what you don't like about yourself is longer than what you do like, it's time to explore where the self-hatred is coming from. Until you love yourself, ultimately you won't be able to let anybody else love you either.

9. Do you think you have to be beautiful or perfect-looking to get love? This is not the case. In fact, often it's just the opposite. In my experience, it's much easier for healthy people with average looks to meet someone nice, marry a faithful spouse, and have children. Several gorgeous male and female acquaintances of mine are still alone in their forties and fifties, having never married or moved in with anyone. This might have to do with having too many choices, ludicrous expectations, or the fact that beautiful people can often skate by on their looks. Yet beauty, or lack of beauty, does not have to hinder love. You can learn to develop other talents and skills to compensate and surprise people's expectations.

10. Do you have strong religious, community, career, charity, or psychological advisers? If you're going through a

rough time, write down who you can go to for straight talk, helpful criticism, and honest answers. Is it a parent, sibling, rabbi, priest, reverend, best friend, teacher, confidante, guru, boss, colleague, manager, accountant, doctor, or therapist? The only prerequisites are that you trust and look up to a person who is willing to listen and advise you. Spend as much time as possible with the kind of people you want to be like. Whenever you're in doubt, emulate those whom you admire. The more mentors you can list, the better. The Psychic Hot Line, the Home Shopping Network, and *Seinfeld* reruns do not count as spiritual fulfillment.

11. Are you finished with past romantic entanglements? If you feel lonely and daydream about one, two, or three of your exes, write yes. If you feel lonely and still sleep with one, two, or three of your exes, kick them out of your bed and call one of the aforementioned advisers. If you don't have one, find someone smart and happily married to talk to—quick.

12. Do you know if you want to have children? Responding yes, no, or "I'd like to try at some point" is a good indicator. Answering "I don't know" or "I have no idea" is a problem, especially for people over thirty-five. If you don't know, who does? Can you at least write down what the decision is dependent on? ("A stable marriage" is a good answer. "Tons of money and nannies" is not so good.)

13. Do you know exactly what pleases you sexually? Were you and your last partner both capable of having an orgasm? I am constantly astounded by how many intelligent, sophisticated men and women I meet who confide that both sides of their current or previous partnership could not climax. As my late friend the

sex therapist Helen Singer Kaplan once told me: "If a female can't come through masturbation alone, she may not be able to climax with her mate." Not yet knowing how to pleasure yourself is nothing to be ashamed of or shy about. It's something that can easily be solved. There are many great sex therapists, erotic toys, videos, and books that can help you.

I myself, the queen of confession, who was proud to publish two brutally honest memoirs my mother hates, had trouble admitting my sexual fantasies to my beloved husband. Luckily my trusted psychoanalyst challenged my reluctance to open up to my spouse. "So are you planning to have affairs or just be sexually unsatisfied for the rest of your life?" he asked. Wow! That semisarcastic question really struck me. Then he took it even further by asking, "How do you think it makes a husband feel when he can't please his wife?" The thought that my shyness and fear of revealing my fantasies could be hurting my mate's feelings and his self-esteem, as well as marring my marriage, convinced me to take the plunge. I divulged intimate secrets to my spouse, asking him to play out sexual scenarios that turned me on.

I admit that it was not easy. We were both nervous and uncomfortable at first (all change is difficult), but he agreed to try. That disclosure wound up being downright transformative and it unlocked everything. Since then, our sex life has never been hotter, our marriage has never been stronger, and—an interesting side effect of our newfound closeness—our separate careers have really been heating up too.

Ready-for-True-Romance Test Results

If you could not answer yes to most of these questions, you are probably not yet ready for a matchmaker or a match. Even if a supertalented setter-upper introduces you to Mr. or Ms. Right, and you wind up married to an amazing partner, there's a good chance you'll blow it somewhere down the line. That's because you have major deficiencies in your life that you will unrealistically expect your partner to fill.

I'm not talking about being faultless here. You don't have to have your issues completely ironed out before you are worthy of being set up on dates. Residences, jobs, luck, friendships, spiritual and psychological needs, weight, habits, and the desire for children can fluctuate anyway. Perhaps just taking the test, questioning yourself, and keeping a journal of your progress will make you think longer and deeper about why you don't have what you want, and how to get it.

What's important is not where you are standing this very second, but that you make the decision to go in a better direction tomorrow morning. Small changes can often lead to bigger and better changes. Many times I have witnessed how little moves can reverse someone's mood and marital status. If you are open-minded and willing to adjust your actions and modify some of your long-term misconceptions, you will be making your matchmaker's job easier—and maybe even unnecessary.

3

MAKING THE MOVE TO IMPROVE

Getting ready for the real thing does not mean you have to be perfect, spend ten years in therapy, exercise four hours a day, complete a Ph.D., or relocate to Alaska (where it is said of the single men "the odds are good, but the goods are odd"). To greatly improve your chances for true love, you merely have to increase your self-love. Make a decision to discover your own priorities and further develop your personal passions. It could start with a positive step as small as:

Plan a Trip or a Special Adventure: After a breakup in her thirties, my fellow University of Michigan alumnus Randye Zerman decided that instead of chasing after another man, she would chase a different dream. She planned a trip to Poland to research the roots of her late grandmother. When a coworker of Randye's mentioned Randye's new obsession to her doctor friend Mark, he was intrigued, since Mark's family also came from Poland. He wanted to meet her. Mark is now Randye's husband and the father of their two children. So one voyage to understand her past altered Randy's future.

Switch the Scenery: Even a two-week vacation somewhere new or a summer house share can be a transforming experience. My close friend Serena Richards, a corporate lawyer, and my former student Beth Lee Segal, a designer, were both single around the time they turned forty. Instead of sitting home moping or pining away for a fantasy guy, each decided to have fun with friends and joined different summer houses in the Hamptons. Perhaps because of their good spirit and independent attitudes, they met Roger and Mitch, and soon married them. Turns out they only had to travel two hours to find husbands who—interestingly—both lived close to them in the city!

Get in Shape: Joining a sports team, trying a new gym, or taking a twice-a-week yoga class could revamp your body, looks, state of mind, and/or energy level. You could meet somebody by literally taking action just one time. Jan, a scientist I know, originally met her partner Evan when she decided to go for a swim at their apartment pool. Come to think of it, Serena met her guy, Roger, in a pool and Beth met her man, Mitch, at the beach. Brains, wit, and integrity are important traits—but if you have a good body you take good care of, showing it off in a bathing suit never hurts.

Get Your House in Order: After Jan and Evan had been dating three years, she felt frustrated that he hadn't proposed. She was sick and tired of waiting around. So she figured forget it and, without him, bought herself a nice little house she'd been eyeing in Ann Arbor. She lovingly fixed it up and redecorated. Just watching someone make accomplishments and move on can motivate another person to wake up and move on too. In this case, Evan took notice, proposed to Jan, and wound up moving into that lovely house as her husband.

Go Back to School: Whether it's returning to get that degree you never finished, or just signing up for a night class in a new subject, getting smarter can't be stupid. If you already have your master's degree or Ph.D., or years of professional experience, consider trying a brand-new subject, or teaching one night a week, to give back and get back too.

If you are overextended or tight for time or money, you can seek out one-shot panels, tutorials, or lectures on nights or weekends. Erica Kennedy, a former New School student of mine, attended an evening seminar Mediabistro.com gave on how to start your novel, which cost twenty-five dollars. Erica started her first fiction project the next day, followed the teacher's instructions, and soon finished and sold *Bling*, her fabulous first book, to Miramax. Erica then met with a graphic designer to help with her book cover— and they've been dating for the last two years! So attending one two-hour seminar led Erica to a great book, a great boyfriend, and basically changed her whole life. Here's to adult education!

Quit an Addiction: Try Alcoholics Anonymous, Narcotics Anonymous, Weight Watchers, the nicotine patch, an addiction specialist, or quit your compulsion cold turkey. Stopping smoking helped me get much healthier, which changed my entire energy level and outlook for four years and counting. Not to mention that these meetings are often swarming with potential new suitors who might understand what you're going through. Indeed, one of my old college roommates met her husband in rehab.

Become a Member: Try out a theater group, a weekly writing workshop, a chess club, or the PTA. Get on your co-op board, chair a committee, or consider joining a union at work or school. You'll meet new people and become part of the community. Aaron originally struck up a conversation with our matchmaker Valerie when they were both on the Writers Guild strike line. Three different women met their matches at my weekly writing workshop. One of them wasn't even a regular member—she just came a few times to check it out.

Reconsider Religious Affiliations: When I lived in Michigan, I became a member of B'nai B'rith youth organization to go to socials and meet other singles. There I wound up introducing my fellow Aliyah-BBG member Nancy Newman to her husband, Jeff Adler. They remain happily united with three adorable children. Years later, when I freelanced for UJA-Federation, a charity organization, a colleague there set me up with a man I dated for two years. Note: I am not proselytizing or suggesting that you find religion—I am not traditional in any way. Yet sometimes merely being among your tribe, in an altruistic setting, makes blessings more likely to happen. My former student Connie Kirk decided to try a different church in a new neighborhood and met Ken Arnold, the handsome ordained deacon who is now her husband. Ken wound up being the publisher of my charity anthology *Food for the Soul*, so now we all go to heaven!

Volunteer and Support Charities: Offer to be a big brother or big sister, help feed the hungry, bring sick or elderly people or children good cheer. These are marvelous ways to meet other kind people and keep good karma circulating. At a benefit reading for that anthology *Food for the Soul* at Holy Apostles church, I introduced Aaron's friend Andy to my former student Trish, a pretty Irish Jew who moved to New York to study Italian. They wound up dating. Since they were both Jewish, Andy and Trish enjoyed telling people they'd met at church. So don't just reconsider your own religion. Be open-minded and check out somebody else's religious charity events too.

Relocate: Move to a new city, a new apartment, or a new house in a new neighborhood, or get a new job or internship. My old college roommate Susie and her sister Ellen were not getting exactly what they wanted when it came to their careers or love lives in Manhattan. When Ellen gave up filmmaking to be a social worker in Northampton, Massachusetts, she met her match in Sam. She now has a thriving practice, a great husband, and three kids. Susie went from part-time researcher in the West Village to full-time newspaper journalist on the West Coast. There she met her husband, had a son, and started winning major newspaper awards. Two years ago, my Michigan protégée Sherry took an unpaid internship at a hip Manhattan weekly. Soon she got her first full-page published clip and an offer for a full-time paying job there. Then she met Danny, a wonderful, kind editor, who is now her boyfriend. Often moving somewhere different leads to different results.

Journal or Blog: Sometimes just writing down what's going on inside you and making a list of issues you want to solve, things you hate or feel gratitude for, and your future goals and aspirations can change your perceptions. Virginia Woolf said, "I write to find out what I think." Ron, a smart member of one of my writing workshops, started blogging and was offered a monthly job as a columnist for a national magazine. Eli, a former student of my husband's, created a comic blog that caught the eye of my agent—who just sold it as a book. My former student Helaine wrote a great essay that was published in the *New York Times* about the disturbance she felt reading her nanny's blog. (Warning: Helaine chronicled firing the nanny—so beware of trashing your employer in a public forum if you plan to keep collecting that paycheck.)

Call a Therapist: My midwestern father and brother Brian used to make sarcastic jokes about my psychoanalysis. That was until my smart shrink, Fred Woolverton, helped me nail a real estate deal that left me with the most valuable home of anybody in my family. Then my dad and Brian called to talk about interest rates and investments. My point is that therapy is not just an elite East and West Coast phenomenon for minor emotional issues. It can help you change any aspect of your life that you feel needs fixing. If there's a stigma against therapy in your small town, fight against it. When in a jam, even the Chicago-based Oprah needed the help of Dr. Phil, that funny post-Freudian Texan. Dr. Woolverton recently moved and now has a thriving practice in Fayetteville, Arkansas.

For the record, successful luminaries who have battled different kinds of depression include Abe Lincoln, William Styron, Elaine Stritch, Ted Turner, Brooke Shields, Daphne Merkin, and Jane Pauley. There are many ways to get professional aid and advice, and it does not have to be expensive. Some helpers (like college counselors) have sliding scales, and some health insurance plans cover specific treatments (like addiction therapy), so expert advice could cost as little as twenty dollars a session. Sometimes just three or four appointments could assist you in refocusing your plans and make a huge difference in your future.

Be Friendlier to Everyone: My friend Lisa Smith, a gregarious social worker, saw a cute man standing on the train platform. Single and in her thirties, Lisa decided not to be shy and let the moment pass. She asked him what time the train arrived. After he answered, she noticed his arm was in a cast and also inquired, "How did you break your arm?" Inside the train, he asked if he could sit with her, said his name was Gerry, worked in the sports business, and totally charmed her. By the time she reached her destination, she knew she wanted to marry him. She did, two years later. Gerry is now her cherished husband and father of her daughter.

Revamp Your Appearance: Ask a stylish pal, classmate, or relative you trust to help you get a makeover. Consider different hair or clothes, contact lenses instead of glasses or different-shaped frames, makeup, eyebrows, manicure, or pedicure. When I invited over several single men to a party my friend Katy was giving, I showed up early and inspected her outfit: an unflattering smock dress and beige flats. I insisted she change and picked out a tight black number hiding in the back of her closet, along with black high heels. I put her hair down and added some sexy makeup. It's no wonder that Jeremy, one of the men I invited, swooned over Katy that night, and wound up marrying her.

Similarly, I recently asked my friend Tim not to wear old blue jeans, sneakers, and a baseball cap to a singles cocktail party I was throwing. He said that I was too superficial. I argued that the event was dressier, and that I couldn't see the benefit of a forty-year-old man dressing like he was twelve. Tim finally acquiesced and showed up looking handsome and spiffy in nice slacks and a sport jacket. That night he met Leslie, a woman he sparked to and went out with twice. He recently told me that Leslie was "one of the smartest, most fascinating people I've ever met." Yes, it's superficial, but in real life first impressions count.

Try a Totally New Type: Open yourself up to different ages, looks, heights, races, religions, professions, and/or backgrounds than you usually go for. Neither of my friends Serena and Beth had originally wanted divorced men with children. Serena was at first dismayed to learn that Roger had been twice divorced, with two grown kids. Similarly, Beth didn't love Mitch's stats and feared his two daughters wouldn't like her or fit into her lifestyle. Luckily Serena and Beth both decided to be more flexible and keep an open mind.

Serena, who married Roger when she was forty-one, told me, "I feel so lucky now that I get to be with a warm, loving person on a day-to-day basis." Their wedding was September 7, 2001. Right after, they left for their honeymoon in Turkey. Four days later nine workers from her office at the World Trade Center were killed and many others were injured. "So, in a sense, Roger's love saved me," Serena added wistfully. Beth, who wed for the first time at age forty-five, recently offered a great follow-up to her big day. "I now think the best perk of my marriage is that I'm so close to Mitch's daughters," she admitted. "I didn't give birth to my own children. But I'm so glad I get to be a mom and grandmother anyway."

Force Yourself to Go to More Social Events: You never know when that soiree, salon, art opening, or charity benefit will bring you closer to that special someone. My colleague Marilyn first spied her husband, Bob, at a book party, as did Barry and my architect friend Cara, who have been an item for over a year now. One of the married couples I fixed up, Rich and Ivy, met at a singles dinner I threw at a local café. Here's my favorite part: Ivy told me she was in a really bad mood that night and definitely did not want to go out. But she pushed herself to change into nicer clothes and shlep downtown. Rich was seated next to her. When she told the person on her other side that she was looking for a drummer for her band Dead Boyfriends, Rich interrupted to say he was a drummer. That drummer became her husband.

Serious note to singles out there who are lonely: the only person you will ever meet while sitting in your living room watching television is a fantasy lover. For real partners you must take a shower, put on nice clean clothes, and leave your house immediately. Even when you would prefer to be shoving ice cream into your mouth while watching TV. Even in the winter!

Start Listening to Your Helpful Mother: My mother's Michigan friend Betty was worried about Ivan, her twenty-eight-year-old son, who'd just moved to Manhattan. Even though I was older, married, and in a different field, she told him to call me to make a new friend. When he did, I invited Ivan over and introduced him to some of my younger East Coast pals, including Ingrid, a former star student of mine also in her twenties. Both smart, political-minded, and adventurous, the two hit it off. They just came back from a year of traveling the world together.

Stop Listening to Your Not-Helpful Mother: Sherry, the hardworking protégée who landed an internship at a hip downtown magazine, was from an Orthodox Jewish family. They didn't approve of Danny, the wonderful, kind, half-Jewish editor she was seeing. Sherry wasn't crazy about Manhattan, or her parents' close-minded insistence that she marry an Orthodox guy. She followed her heart and she and Danny are now madly in love and living together in Chicago.

Invite a Different Crowd of New People to Your Next Party: My friend Linda, a mother of two who works in real estate, was going through a rough divorce. She wasn't meeting anybody new and special while hanging out with married couples, her kids' playmates' moms, or her divorced circle. So Linda asked me to help her throw a New Year's party. She offered to pay for all the food and alcohol and said that I could invite all of my single cronies to eat and drink. Good deal for me! I was thrilled to oblige, we had a swell soiree, and it's no coincidence that Linda is now getting serious with my colleague Terry, a best-selling author. That New Year's party was also where I originally met Lisa's friend Cara, the architect (now dating Barry). Linda and Cara joke that because of that one social event they both wound up with marvelous men, whose names rhyme.

Change Your Attitude and the Way You Connect: My former classmate Georgia Hill met Michael at a youth group called the Young Adult Ministry in Detroit. She had decided to switch her career from attorney to minister. She was attracted to Michael, a good-looking financial planner who by coincidence lived in her apartment building. When he saw her dressed up and looking gorgeous at church one day, he asked, "What would it take to whisk you off to an island?" She pointed to her ring finger and said, "Marriage." She had decided, in her thirties, to reorganize her priorities. She no longer wanted to share intimacy with men who didn't deserve her affection. She figured that if Michael cared enough, he would wait. You know what? He waited. After dating sex-free for one year they consummated their relationship on their honeymoon.

"Part of the development of my faith was realizing that I did not have to settle," Georgia told me. "It was important that I learned to trust and value myself, stick to my guns. Now I tell young people, if somebody isn't treating you right, you don't have to tolerate that nonsense. You should wait to find someone who treats you the way you deserve to be treated."

Amen.

4

WHO MAKES A GOOD MATCHMAKER?

Let's say you aced the Ready-for-True-Romance test. Or maybe you flunked, but you're working on getting your head, act, apartment, friendships, immediate family connections, and/or job scene together. So you've been making minor changes in your world by: saving up for a special vacation adventure, consulting a therapist, signing up for a new class, and/or updating your résumé for a better job. That's fabulous. Can't you just feel the positive energy flowing? If not, just lie and pretend you can. Nobody but shrinks want to deal with a negative, depressed person— and they only do it for the paycheck.

The next step is finding your matchmaker. But before you ask anyone to fix you up, you have to make sure you will be approaching the right person, for the right reasons. Pull out your notebook, and on an empty page write a list of everyone in your life you know well, feel comfortable with, trust, look up to, and admire. If your list contains more than thirty names, you can narrow it down by putting a star next to the ones who appear to be happily coupled. More likely you can only come up with two or three. So consider the following groups.

Your Crazy Clan: Yes, I know the whole beauty of marriage is that you'll finally get to choose somebody you'll be related to. But believe it or not, many relatives are excellent fixer-uppers. Although I spent my childhood screaming at my loud and rambunctious kid brother, Brian, I wound up hooking him up with his wife (and mother of his four gorgeous kids). My friend Judy was set up with her fantastic lawyer husband, Jim Burdick, by a distant cousin. Marilyn, a Long Island designer I know, was introduced to the man she married by her father. Family members who stand to benefit most by your marriage just might be worth listening to.

Coworkers: How many employees work at your office? Ten? Fifty? Two hundred? Since you hopefully enjoy what you do, and you spend forty to sixty hours every week there, this is an excellent place for career-minded singles to look for a love network. You'll probably be attending the same meetings, presentations, award ceremonies, and holiday parties as the rest of the staff. This gives you a common bond with your office mates, underlings, and fellow worker bees. So starting conversations should be natural and easy. When you are standing by the elevator, saying something as mundane as, "Can you believe Jim in accounting is leaving after twenty years?" or, "I'm so glad we get the week of Christmas off. Aren't you?" can break the ice.

If your job station is hidden away in a far-off cubicle, you are shy, or are the only young single person on your floor, there are many ways to get to know more people on the job and stand out as someone special. You can offer to serve on a committee, volunteer to be in charge of secret Santas, or organize a shower for a pregnant coworker. It can also be endearing when you remember people's names, bring in baked goods for your department to share, send casual New Year's greetings, birthday cards, or Valentines, and compliment colleagues on their nice clothes or good energy. To cultivate a closer connection, look up someone's previous work, awards, publications, achievements, or background and express interest. I know it sounds simple or cheesy. Yet there are so many negative, bitter souls one encounters daily that spreading a little kindness and flattery can work wonders. Especially if it's specific, tactful, and thoughtfully rendered.

After I taught a weekend seminar, Sally, a young woman who attended, sent me a card that said "I wanted to thank you for being so warm, helpful, and generous. I was very inspired by you and went out and bought your book. I hope you'll sign it for me." I e-mailed her back that same day, invited her to come to meet a *New York Times* editor speaking at my next class (for free), and offered to read and edit an article she was rewriting. All because she had the good sense to express gratitude for my efforts!

As a freelancer, I met with as many as two hundred different clients in one year. Although I didn't have much money at the time, I would send editors little chocolate ghosts on Halloween, dreidels on Hannukah, and colored confetti for New Year's. I always wrote thank-you notes to anybody who went out of their way for me. My tiny acts of emotional generosity were often appreciated, reciprocated, and rewarded. It's no wonder I went out of my way to find spouses for my favorite boss Jasmine (when I was her subordinate at a nonprofit agency), my coworker Monica (when we both were peons at *The New Yorker* magazine's editorial library), and my editor Dina (when we worked on two books together).

Trusted Staff: My sister-in-law Carol met her adored husband, Gary Kahn, through the hairdresser they both shared. I invited my architect Cara to the book event where she met her boyfriend (who was the brother of Emma, my old *New Woman* editor). Examine others on your payroll, including stylists, accountants, real estate brokers, bankers, personal trainers and shoppers, and yoga instructors, doctors, dentists, and therapists. They know you well, probably like you, and might even feel invested in your happiness and potential gratitude. If you ask, the worst they'll say is, "Sorry, can't think of anyone." But you will put it in their mind and they might come back to you later. At best, they'll hook you up, knowing they could gain more of your business and/or another customer.

Adult Education: Kim, one of the star students from my NYU feature-writing class, wound up with an "A" grade, a magazine clip, a good recommendation, and a steady boyfriend, Paul, whom she's still seeing three years later. If you are in any kind of degree program or even just taking a few classes or seminars on the side, consider asking classmates, students, principals, heads of your department, guidance counselors, and/or favorite teachers. If it feels too intimate, wait until you graduate, finish the semester, or end the class. It's never a bad idea to start with (honest) flattery, as in, "Since you were my favorite teacher" or, "Listen, you're the person I trust most here . . ."

Work Mentors: Since I looked up to my freelance employers Emma and Valerie, who were both older than I and married, they became my ideal matchmakers. Emma was the one who coughed up the charming shrink Joshua for me—at a business lunch she insisted on paying for. I met Valerie when I worked as her assistant, typing her two-hundred-page screenplay. I toiled twenty-four hours straight so she could make her deadline, and we soon became friends. After she started a conversation and asked if I was single, I said yes. Then I took a chance and threw out, "If you know any great single guys, keep me in mind." That one-line inquiry led to my marriage. The squeaky wheel does get the grease, so don't be shy and squeakless.

Don't be afraid to pursue those you look up to. At lunch, on break, or before or after work, inquire how your married superiors met their spouses, and solicit their opinion on the best way to find a partner. Consider asking your agent, editor, producer, manager, or head of your department (though in private, when you're sure it's their downtime too, of course). Group leaders and bosses often love giving advice and being looked up to. That's usually why they choose positions of authority in the first place.

Neighbors: While exchanging pleasantries with the nice couple that lives next door, let them know you're single and looking not to be. Ditto the manager of the deli where you overtip every day, and the owners of the local bookstore you frequent. (If they recall everyone's taste in food and reading material, they might know more than you think.) The superintendent of your building and your doormen already protect you. Plus they know who is single, screwing around, who pays their bills on time, and who is a deadbeat. Don't underestimate geographical desirability, especially if you don't want to move, are lazy, and don't have the money, time, or inclination to travel.

Old Friends and Fans: Carly, a Texas flight attendant, stayed in touch with her high school boyfriend's mother, even after the ex in question married. Always regretting that Carly hadn't married her son—and perhaps feeling guilty that he had broken up with her—this almost mother-in-law wound up setting up Carly with her future husband.

Any devotee should be appreciated and cultivated. Accept support where it is offered—especially from people who knew you back when, in your old hometown.

Recycled Romance: I admit it—I had first dates with three of the men I wound up setting up with their wives. They were all great guys—they just weren't great for me. If you are kind and gentle about it, there is nothing wrong with asking former flames to fix you up or vice versa. This is especially true if you remained platonic with your onetime partner, you are currently lonely, and they are now harmoniously married with children. If this ex was the one who split up with you—even better. A little guilt can go a long way. I heard of one scenario where a former husband attempted to set up his first wife to get out of paying alimony. I say there's nothing wrong with added motivation. Okay, it can be awkward to first float the idea out there. But hey, never look a gift match in the mouth.

Who Usually Makes a Bad Matchmaker

Someone you don't like or who you suspect doesn't really like you

Someone with a partner you don't like

Someone you don't trust and wouldn't tell a secret to

Someone with a spouse you don't trust, whom you wouldn't want to know any of your secrets

Someone unhappily single, miserably married, or multiply divorced

Someone merely miserable, since miserable people tend to like people to be as miserable as they are

Someone who agrees to set you up while coming on to you

5

WHY MATCHMAKERS ARE GOOD LOVE MENTORS

Once you've expanded your list of potential matchmakers, cross off anybody unhelpful or snobbish who makes you feel bad about yourself, and forget anybody in a love partnership you don't respect. Now it's time to approach the good, nice people you like, see often, and admire. Embarrassing as it can be, you must explicitly let them know that you are unattached and searching for someone serious. The exact words you use will count. When I was in my twenties, I would be subtle and say to a pal, "Hey, your neighbor Nick is cute. What's his story?" That got me nowhere. (Okay, maybe it got me laid, but that led nowhere.) When I was in my thirties and ready for the real thing with the ring, I told Emma and Valerie: "I'm sick of Romeos and Peter Pans. I'm only looking for husband material." *That* got me two matchmakers. And they got me married.

Ever since I became an older, married person, I think older, married people make the best matchmakers. Yet I fixed up quite a few couples when I was young, solo, and screwed up. So if somebody younger, single, or somewhat crazy happens to be sociable, what the hell, let them fix you up too. People are often better with other people's lives than their own. Be open. Teenagers can fix up the elderly, gays can set up straights, Muslims can introduce WASPs and vice versa. The moment you make the decision to share your desire for a mate, the world will conspire to help you. Still, whom you choose to ask, the place and time you do it, your manner, and your specific phrasing will determine whether you strike out or have success recruiting guardian angels to get you love.

Do not start this intricate and important process by throwing the idea out casually, in the middle of a movie, party, meeting, or phone call about something else. You need to have a one-on-one conversation. Ask the person you want to set you up out for breakfast, lunch, dinner, a drink, or a quiet walk. If that's too intimate to ask of a new boss or colleague, or the person seems too busy, suggest a brief meeting. You can stop by his or her office, home, or somewhere else convenient for your potential fixer-upper. If it's a long-distance friend, say, "I have something I'd like to ask you. What's a good time to call when I won't be interrupting anything?" You might want to make a joke that you don't want to borrow money.

Sometimes it's best to make a phone appointment in advance and then make sure you call at exactly that time. You can also carefully craft an appropriate—though short—note, letter, card, or e-mail. "Hey, Joe, your cousin Lisa has a hot bod. Want to hook us up?" will only be effective if you want someone you admire to think you are a frat-boy bozo. Instead, try something earnest and corny, to the effect of: "David, I really admire your relationship with your wonderful wife, Angela. This is a little awkward to admit, but I'm feeling ready to meet someone special. I wondered if

Angela might have any single girlfriends as warm and beautiful as she is."

In fact, starting the conversation slowly with (believable) flattery rarely fails. For example, over lunch with a coworker you'd like to cultivate as a matchmaker, say, "Gayle, can I ask you something personal?" If she says yes, continue with, "Your husband sounds like such a great guy. How did you two meet?" You don't necessarily have to formally inquire—or get a definite response—as to whether Gayle or Joe will be your official matchmaker. You can say, "Keep me in mind if you come across anybody single who you think is special." It's like networking for a job or an apartment. Often someone will say, "I'll think about it," "I'll ask around," or, "I'll keep you in mind" and then get back to you if something comes up. Following up after a few weeks—or a few months—is not a bad idea, though obviously hounding someone unresponsive is not cool. You certainly don't want your potential matchmaker to think you're too hyper, desperate, or a stalker.

Even if you are sharing confidences with your best bar buddy, remember that the labels you use are important and will convey your intentions. You are no longer looking for a fling, fun time, one-night stand, one-time date, cute arm candy, or pal with privileges. You want to intersect with someone special, an admirable person who might become your most important immediate family member and perhaps the parent of your future children. Start having respect for the institution right now.

Opening up and sharing your vulnerability could make your matchmaker understand you and care for you more. Admitting that you've been lonely, or had a hard time at your kid sister's wedding and baby shower, or never quite got over your last love affair that ended two years before, are acceptable and appropriate admissions to make when you're alone with someone you respect. If you throw in flattery and admiration, it can be an engaging, endearing opening that will forge a deeper connection. Min-Li, a pretty thirty-four-year-old journalism student of mine, slipped me a typed note at our final session last semester. She apologized for missing a few classes and assignments, explaining that she was preoccupied from a recent painful breakup. She added that my book about my breakups, *Five Men Who Broke My Heart*, had been consoling her. Shoshana, another female student in her early thirties, also told me about her love troubles in a long e-mail. She'd moved out of her not-so-fabulous-sounding boyfriend's place, but she was still seeing him and confused about her next step. She repeated lines I'd said about therapy (yes, I've been known to babble about it openly and constantly in class) and wanted my advice.

I took Shoshana to lunch, gave her a few little presents (including soaps and shampoos to help you "wash your old boyfriend out of your hair"), and asked more about what was going on. I basically agreed with her therapist and encouraged her to keep her shrink but dump the guy. We now speak on the phone and e-mail on a regular basis. I thought of a few nice guys I would love her to meet—but not until she can untangle herself from her ex. I also got together with Min-Li outside of class and introduced her to Mike, my cute friend close to her age who works at the bookstore across the street.

Many students have made gestures to befriend me, talk to me before or after class, or have outside meetings. A few even point-blank asked me to write them graduate school recommendations, edit more of their work, or become their mentors. Several former pupils invited me to holiday parties and readings they were giving. One even invited me to have dinner with her and her parents, who were in from out of town. I politely declined 99 percent of these invitations, since I'm often on deadline and overburdened with class-work. Yet I responded warmly to Shoshana and Min-Li, and made time for them. How did they slip through my busy schedule and barriers? They approached me in unobtrusive ways that made reaching out to them easier.

Unlike many others, neither woman approached me when I was busy, couldn't focus, and felt put upon. It stuns me how many times someone will come up to me in the ten minutes I have in between two big classes, when forty people are shuffling in and out, and start asking me for help with a long personal story. I was able to read Min-Li's typed note and Shoshana's e-mail after class and on my own time, when I wasn't harried or overwhelmed with work. Both missives were very flattering. They both also revealed that they were struggling with romantic problems, but they didn't share too much information or details. An honest yet classy approach will make people want to help you.

Unless you are talking to a close friend who has known and loved you forever, or a family member, don't confess all of your sins right off the bat. You will have better luck first using discretion, humility, and a little bit of restraint. Think carefully before telling your potential matchmaker about your previous abortions, drug addictions, and/or deviant sexual escapades. If this person was your roommate in college and already knows your whole dubious past, I wouldn't even bring up the time you wound up sleeping in your car, naked, or getting arrested.

Important exceptions: if you are being—or have been—mistreated, raped, abused, hurt, or drugged, or are in any way strung-out, homeless, broke, ill, depressed, suicidal, or being stalked or threatened by anyone, please do confide in a trusted teacher, adviser, older ally, relative, or family friend as soon as possible. Do not underestimate the impact these troubles can have on your psyche. I have been happy to connect many people with counselors, doctors, and other professionals. Several young students have approached me to fix them up with dates when, after a longer conversation, what they really need is a therapist, doctor, lawyer, real estate agent, college or graduate school adviser, or career counselor first. Initiating contact and closeness with a trusted person can really help with many things that might need mending.

When you click with a matchmaker who might be interested in matching you, try not to spill your deep desires for material wealth, models, mansions, willingness to try certain sex acts, and preference for the size or shape of specific body parts. Bling, hot abs, and sexual chemistry appear to be essential elements of seduction in certain movies and music videos. Yet in real life, the less specific and materialistic your request, the better. Would you rather get on board to push a sex-crazed gold digger toward a rich filmmaker, or help a lonely friend find someone sweet to take her to dinner? If you must be superficial, have as few external requirements as possible, and relay the areas where you have wiggle room.

When I was single and someone asked what kind of guy I could see myself with, I admit that I answered "a tall, smart, funny guy who reads." Luckily in my social circles, that turned out to be findable. This was partly because I was flexible when it came to other traits—differences in age, education, weight, the way he dressed, the kind of place where he lived, and employment. I had a nice apartment, fantastic colleagues and friendships, plus two careers I loved and planned to work at forever. So I wasn't desperate for someone who could supply the living quarters, social life, professional connections, or financial stability that I'd already managed to find myself.

By my thirties I'd learned that no partner was ever going

to have every single fantasy quality or common trait I'd imagined. I no longer expected someone I was dating to be my best friend, confidant, family, shrink, editor, and business adviser. (That's why we have best friends, confidants, family, shrinks, editors, and business advisers.) I was a complete person with a complete life, and it was quite liberating to not burden a lover with too many unrealistic expectations. It's much easier to get what you need when you don't need everything in one person.

When I was ready to go for it, I put the word out to my extended circle loudly, and more than once. Yes, I felt dumb and weird to confess that I was lonely and apparently incapable of attracting a decent date on my own. But when somebody expressed interest in my quest or asked me more questions, I acted enthusiastic, positive, and grateful. (Offering to pick up the check for lunch and/or giving a little present, like a book or CD, isn't a bad idea either.) Since at the time I was writing twisted confessional poetry like a Sylvia Plath wannabe, I consciously refrained from being critical, cynical, morbid, ironic, snide, and negative. Instead I did my best to come off sane, strong, healthy, and happy. Why? Would you want to marry somebody trying to emulate Sylvia Plath? Would you fix up your brother with someone who could be a bulimic cutter?

I was not denying my inner rage or darkness. I was merely indulging the part of my personality that was upbeat, cheerful, healthy, and hardworking, as I would in a graduate school, job, or co-op board interview. Most important, I was open-minded. I agreed to meet any guys for a drink whom my matchmakers deemed special, kind, nice, or menschy— even if they were short, gray-haired, bald, unemployed, fashion challenged, too thin or too fat, or not known for their sense of humor. I dated men of all races, religions, backgrounds, and career aspirations. My good attitude was part of the reason why so many friends and colleagues agreed to assist me. (Or maybe I guilted them into it with all the sincere flattery, picking up lunch tabs and those little presents.)

I knew how to act because I had also been on the other side of the table, setting up singles myself. I was often turned off immediately by the stubborn, solitary type whose attitude came off as closed off, stuck up, angry, materialistic, superficial, pretentious, creepy, needy, excessively picky, hyper, or semi-insane. I recently met Robin, a pretty, smart, fifty-year-old professor who begged me to fix her up. Through a close friend I met Joel, a successful, handsome fifty-five-year-old divorced lawyer. Bingo! I was excited to introduce him to Robin. Within minutes of my mentioning him, Robin e-mailed me these questions: "What kind of law does he practice? Where's his office? Where did he go to law school? How long has he been divorced? Why did he get divorced? Is he still friends with his ex-wife?" I felt like I was doing her a big favor and she was already giving me a big headache. But anybody could get a little antsy or nervous about dating, right?

So I calmly told Robin that I did not know Joel well enough to answer all these questions. But a close girlfriend, whose taste I totally trusted, had given Joel a huge seal of approval. I suggested that Robin chill out, halt the obsessive interrogation, and just have a cup of coffee with Joel before needing to know every single detail of his existence, including at what age he was toilet trained. How many fantastic, single, successful fifty-five-year-old men in her city and right in her neighborhood did she think were out there and interested in meeting her? Unfortunately, Robin e-mailed Joel the same litany of ridiculous questions she'd asked me. After three e-mails he decided that she was too neurotic and never even met her! He did go out with the next woman I hooked him up with, who was easier-going and more restrained. Sorry, but the only people I will ever fix Robin up with again are a shrink, a yoga teacher, or a masseur.

Despite how you really feel deep down, it's a good idea to monitor your requests and responses and act gracious with your matches—and your matchmaker. If the person trying to fix you up gives you advice, try to take it. We are on your side and want you to be happy and bond with your match. If you win, we win. I know that talking about romance and dream partners can bring out people's arrogance and insanity. But often, in the name of misguided honesty, you can be unwittingly estranging the one you need to be in sync with. If you are not aware of how you're coming off, ask your sibling, therapist, or a close friend who is not fixing you up for honest feedback first.

I'm not implying that the opinions of your sibling, close friend, therapist, or matchmaker must always be heard, heeded, and honored. Yet don't instantly spurn any of their suggestions either. Remember, your "my way or the highway" attitude has not served you well in the past. If it worked, you might not be single and struggling with the dating scene right now. So try to listen more closely than usual. Even if your feelings get hurt, write down the advice. Let it sink in before you react, overreact, or alienate potentially important connections. Use a calm, kind tone to respond, smile, and don't interrupt or reject anything too quickly. That doesn't mean that you have to go along with everything they say. But smart, good-natured arguing is underrated. If you don't get it, debate, dispute, cajole, joust, tease, joke, and keep asking questions. That's what close friends, therapists, mentors, and matchmakers are there for.

It amazes me how often singles I barely know will pursue, push, and beg me for fix-ups or party invitations. Then, the minute I try, close-minded refusals, haughty attitude, and self-defeating laziness are what I get in response to my efforts. Here are typical conversations I often have with people who have come to me for advice and dates. After a few wrong or rude responses, I cross someone off my list forever. So slow down and think first next time, before saying no to someone nice who is trying to care, connect, and help you find love.

POTENTIAL MATCHMAKER'S SUGGESTION: A lot of my single friends will be at this fun party I was invited to in Ann Arbor on Saturday night. Want to come with me?

WRONG RESPONSE: Ann Arbor is an hour away from my place. I can't drive that distance for a party. That's too far away.

ESPECIALLY WRONG BECAUSE: Driving one hour to meet new people at a party you were invited to is not unreasonable, especially if you've been complaining you're lonely and the alternative is staying home on yet another Saturday night to eat ice cream, watch television, and call friends to complain how rough it is being single.

RIGHT RESPONSE: Thank you so much for the invitation. It sounds interesting and fun. It's not in my neighborhood. But maybe I'll give it a shot. Can I let you know later?

RIGHT MOVE: Give it a shot! If you are nervous about going to a strange area you don't know, plan to go early and make a fun day out of exploring a new city. Or if you can, carpool with the person who invited you. Or ask if you're allowed to bring another friend so you don't have to travel alone. Or take a cab, bus, train, or try a car service.

VERY WRONG MOVE: If you do go to a neighborhood you don't know, do not take drugs or drink more than one alcoholic beverage. Several recent murders occurred after a single person got plastered on six drinks or drugs in a strange area at four in the morning. Remember to tread carefully in new territory and don't expect people you've never met to have your values. It's much easier to drive, travel, get home, stay alert, and protect yourself when you are clean and sober. If you are the least bit nervous, bring a friend with you and travel in pairs.

POTENTIAL MATCHMAKER'S SUGGESTION: My coworker Alex is really nice, but he's not that tall. I think you might like him, though. Can I introduce you?

WRONG RESPONSE: Oh God, how short is he? I never go out with short men. I'm five foot seven and always wear heels, so if he's not at least five ten, forget it.

ESPECIALLY WRONG BECAUSE: "Not that tall" is subjective. You don't want to rule out half the men on the planet for superficial reasons—plus, your matchmaker's husband, father, or brother could be five foot seven.

RIGHT RESPONSE: Really? He's nice? I'm looking for someone nice. Tell me more about him.

RIGHT MOVE: Agree to meet him, be charming, wear flats, and if he turns out to be short, but nice and interested, try one more time. At least make a new friend.

VERY WRONG MOVE: Do not tell your date directly that he's nice but too short for you. Would you want to hear that you are too fat for somebody? Or too flat chested? Or too old? Or that your nose is too big? If you must share this kind of information, save it for your matchmaker, so he or she knows you need more height in the future.

POTENTIAL MATCHMAKER'S SUGGESTION: I could just give you my friend Sarah's e-mail.

WRONG RESPONSE: I can't just e-mail someone I've never met! I mean, what if I'm not attracted to her? What does she look like? Is she thin? I hate fat women. Do you have a picture?

ESPECIALLY WRONG BECAUSE: Sarah might be beautiful. You don't have to be so negative, nervous, and untrusting. Plus, e-mailing someone new could be a slow and appropriate way of seeing if you two have anything in common before you ask her to get together.

RIGHT RESPONSE: Sure, I'll take your friend Sarah's e-mail address. Thank you for thinking of me. Will you mention to her that I might be contacting her? Tell me more about her.

RIGHT MOVE: Send a sweet, innocuous e-mail with an informal invitation to meet. I'd try something like "I'm a friend of Sue's. She mentioned you also like literary events. I'm going to hear Salman Rushdie read at Barnes & Noble next Tuesday at seven. Any chance you're free and want to meet me?" Readings are a great place to meet someone new. They are often free, interesting, casual, and can last less than an hour. And there's usually a coffee bar you can suggest trying afterward.

VERY WRONG MOVE: Not everyone in the world uses technology like you do. Do not send someone you've never met the long, weird poem about your last breakup that you just composed, instant message him, or put him on your group e-mail list for dumb jokes, political screeds, fund-raising pleas, or chain letters. Also beware of cybersymbols and abbreviations. Some people might not find ☺:) LOL so clear, cute, or endearing.

The process of finding a matchmaker can teach you much about life, love, and success. Many people don't actually know what their goal is, and thus cannot whisper into the right sympathetic ear what they are looking for. Picture what would happen if you needed a job but were too shy to network. (Nothing. Chances are you would remain jobless.) Or if you had no place to live, but decided not to pound the pavement, hoping landlords would read your mind and offer you a new one-bedroom apartment. (You could wind up homeless.) It's much easier to get what you want once you determine exactly what that is and learn how to ask for it.

Once I figured out this formula, I began asking (okay, begging) everyone paired off whom I held in high esteem to lend a hand with my husband hunt. Over a long lunch, I cajoled Emma, my editor at *New Woman* magazine, for another assignment. When she asked if I was seeing someone, I tossed out that I was lonely and asked if she had any great single friends. She recalled that her brother's best pal, the aforementioned psychoanalyst Joshua, was getting divorced. He lived in Baltimore and had two kids, which was not on the top-ten list of what I was looking for in a husband. But Emma assured me that he was honest and smart. So I trusted her, took a chance, and the rest was almost history.

Why Asking to Be Set Up Is Such an Essential Step

- You must decide exactly what you want and ask for it out loud. This will start to demystify, clarify, and define what otherwise could remain a vague and general desire. It will help you begin to strategize about how to attain your goal.

- Sharing your purpose with people in your world whom you care about and trust demands that you figure out whom in your world you care about and trust. Also, initiating this conversation with people you might not yet have confided in involves taking an emotional risk. It could make you feel vulnerable and open, good emotions to lead toward intimacy. Even being spurned by a potential matchmaker could be a helpful experience in learning to handle rejection without overreacting. It's much easier to be rejected by a matchmaker than by a match you like.

- When talking to potential matchmakers, you might have to overcome such limitations as shyness, shame, nervousness, fear, insecurities, and awkwardness discussing intimate details of relationships. Often these are the same blocks you'll have to break through on subsequent dates.

- Deciding you need a matchmaker encourages you to create a larger network and look at people in a different way. It forces you to focus on marriages you admire and want to emulate and pushes you to figure out what qualities you need in a long-term partner.

- Your quest will provide a good excuse for you to get in touch with out-of-touch relatives, old friends, classmates, former bosses, and colleagues. Try a media blitz, where you phone, fax, e-mail, and/or use snail mail. It might take creativity, spunk, and forcefulness to locate everyone.

- You'll have to get more creative socially. If you fear that finding people you haven't seen in a while just to fix you up could be seen as too presumptuous or desperate, then use the excuse that you're throwing a party, hosting a reading, planning a charity benefit, or having an unofficial reunion you want to invite everyone to.

- It's good to put yourself on the line emotionally. It's not so horrible to admit to the crowd from your past that you're going through a rough time. Or changing.

Or transitioning into a new stage. You could come across someone recently divorced or widowed who'd now love to socialize with you. Some people get kinder and wiser as they age and you might be pleasantly surprised. When I was researching a book, I called five ex-boyfriends and basically said, "I'm going through a midlife crisis trying to figure out my past and it would mean a lot if we could have a cup of coffee." Five out of five agreed to talk and all of the conversations were illuminating.

- By asking people you like to fix you up and give you advice, you are cultivating mentors to guide you through a sometimes difficult process. Perhaps their honest answers to your questions will help you penetrate unrealistic myths you have about sex and marriage. Someone who has been a longtime spouse can teach you more about the ins and outs of realistic unions than any Hollywood movie, romance novel, or sexy sitcom. You can hear the real scoop and lose all your unhelpful misconceptions about dating and mating.

- This is your chance to pose embarrassing questions you've always wanted to ask. I was having lunch with a young female student who blurted out, "How did you get such a good husband?" I laughed out loud. Then I told her the truth: good therapist, good matchmaker, a lot of work on myself, then good luck.

- You'll hear how you sound and learn to better describe and edit yourself and your wishes. A pretty forty-five-year-old woman whom I'd just met was asking me to fix her up at a recent holiday party. Listing what she wanted in a guy, she said, "I don't want someone short, fat, out of shape, or much older than me. He has to be smart, successful, and in shape. I have to feel attraction. I do care about looks." Before I could even ask, "Have you considered whether your vanity is self-defeating, hiding fear, and/or keeping you from love?" she stopped herself and said, "I'm not really that superficial. If a guy is smart and nice, I'd be open."

- You're polishing your social skills, tact, and powers of persuasion, trying to cajole and charm a potential matchmaker into seeing you as an ideal suitor for someone they know and care about. You might have to improve your method of communication, define what's special and different about you, and convince others by finding ways to make yourself stand out.

- Even just a consultation with a prospective matchmaker can sometimes be like a free therapy session. Your romantic fantasies reveal a lot about you. A perceptive fixer-upper might uncover a huge flaw in your life plan, priority list, or logic that you weren't conscious of. It's never easy to hear that you should consider getting your schooling, home, family dynamics, addiction issues, body, attitude, or career in order before trying to connect with a soul mate. Yet if the person suggesting this is someone you look up to and want to be like, consider that his or her motive might be to help unlock you.

- Meeting with your matchmaker is a great practice run. Someone on your side who wants you to win will tell you the truth about details you might not notice. Often there are minor mistakes you can fix before alienating any more potential suitors. For example, my friend Alana arrived early to a singles party I was throwing. I was delighted to see her, but aghast to see her long dark hair hiding behind a floral 1950s-looking headband. Big mistake. This dishrag on her head had turned a gorgeous gal with luscious long tresses into an old-fashioned and dowdy-looking schoolmarm and I told her so. Alana said "Screw you," went to the bathroom, took it off, fluffed up her marvelous mane, and met a guy two hours later.

No, you don't always have to meet your match-maker's standards of beauty. But Alana was forty-four, had never been married, was constantly complaining that she was lonely, and was coming to a singles party hosted by a happily married friend who loved her. So the chances were pretty good that I had a point, a fair perspective, insider information (men are superficial and care about looks), as well as excellent motivation. Remember—your matchmaker really, really wants you to be successful, because that makes her successful too!

- Instead of being a loner, tough guy, self-sufficient superwoman, or control freak who can handle everything on your own, you are admitting that you are not an island. Instead you are already asking the right people for help, which is always the first step toward getting it.

6

HOW TO BE FIXED UP
FABULOUSLY

Getting the Right Attitude
and Perspective

It's rare to hit the bull's-eye on the first try of anything. As a freelance writer, I've kept all of my rejection slips over the years. I used to have rejection slip parties for my classes, where I'd tape all of my rebuffs from book, magazine, and newspaper editors on the walls. My favorites were the ones from places that later bought my work. Since I wanted my students to get out there and try to submit their writing professionally, I insisted that the price of admission from each guest was a rejection slip. This way, instead of feeling dejected and alone, everyone could look at getting a first "No, we don't want you" missive as a fun public initiation ritual to be celebrated. Mazel tov! You got out there! You're a real writer now!

Although many students of mine do get published by the end of class, their first drafts almost never see print. Third, fourth, or fifth versions, which tend to be much improved, are the ones that sell. And I often notice that it's not my most intelligent, oldest, or most experienced pupils who wind up getting internships, jobs, and ink. It tends to be the aspirants who work the hardest—crafting the most drafts of the largest number of essays they send to a variety of different editors. Then they follow up—sometimes five or six times. When an editor suggests trying something different, the winners are the ones who comply and compromise.

Recently my student Stacey Kramer started publishing regular fashion pieces for the *New York Sun*. When the editor of their "Style" section spoke to my class, she revealed how Stacey came to be one of her steady writers. Stacey had originally pitched personal essays and author profiles that the editor had no room for. But Stacey did not give up, nor did she take the rebuffs personally. She remained sweet and appreciative, thanking the editor profusely for her time, and asking if there was another area where she might have better luck. "Do you like fashion?" the editor asked Stacey one day. "Sure," Stacey said, though in truth it wasn't her area of expertise or her forte. Still, Stacey was willing to give it a shot and now has ten clips and checks to show for it. The editor told the class that Stacey's delightful demeanor and willingness to compromise were rare. It stood out and made her someone you wanted to help and work with. (Not surprisingly, Stacey is happily married. I'm sure she brought the same enthusiasm and sweetness to her quest for a spouse.)

Over the years, my most successful protégés have been the ones who were willing to try again and again without letting a few "Sorry, this doesn't work for us" responses dampen their energy. The same has been true with fix-ups. It's not the most beautiful, successful, richest, or youngest singles who click with their matches the fastest and have the best marriages. It's the people who are the most open-minded, willing to bend, grow, change, and take lemons and make lemonade—even when they'd prefer vodka and orange juice.

In my fourteen-week journalism overview class, I give thirteen assignments that I edit line by line. I tell my students they can choose to do a revision instead of a new piece each week. One wannabe scribe, Daniel, rewrote the same essay for weeks on end. When he kept reading his rewrites aloud, others balked and teased him. Then Daniel published that piece in the *New York Times Magazine* for a thousand dollars, eclipsing all his classmates. Harvey Shapiro, a *New York Times* editor for fifty years (and no relation), was not surprised by that story. When another student of mine asked Shapiro, "Are the famous writers you first published the ones who had the most talent?" he replied, "No. It was the ones who were the most obsessed."

This is true in most fields. Very few television or film people make a mark in their first movie or TV show. In the 1980s Larry David was broke and out of work. He'd bombed in some stand-up comedy circuits, acted in the obscure movies *Second Thoughts* and *Can She Bake a Cherry Pie?*, worked on the not famous television shows *Norman's Corner* and *Fridays*, and had attempted a few not very illustrious seasons of *Saturday Night Live* before he created *Seinfeld* in 1990, when he was forty-three years old. Many fans focus on the result and forget that it took three seasons for the award-winning sitcom to take off.

Sometimes it takes talented artists even longer for recognition. I loved when Holland Taylor, a wonderful actress in her sixties, won her first Emmy for her work on the TV drama *The Practice* forty years into her theater, film, and television career. On stage she held up her statue and quipped, "An overnight success!" to thunderous applause.

The insightful nonfiction book *Getting It Right the Second Time*, by Michael Gershman, chronicles how such products as LifeSavers, ballpoint pens, Post-it Notes, vacuum cleaners, Cracker Jack, Wisk, 7Up, and Vaseline all initially failed on the market. Then, with more work, renaming, repackaging, and other informed improvements, all later became huge megasellers. The same can be said of the quest for a spouse. It's a process, and attitude counts for everything. Try not to look at it as a painful excursion or competition, but as a fascinating voyage that might involve a lot of revision and rejection along the way. In order not to quit or burn out, you have to keep improvising and improving, and learning more about yourself and what you need. My particular love and career history could be called "Getting It Right the Hundredth Time."

There are ways to brainwash yourself into being sanguine and serene during the times of search and struggle. Keep your expectations in check. Try to always err on the side of generosity. Be conscious of karma and treat others the way you want to be treated. And remember: the purpose of dating is so you'll never have to date again. Instead of "crossing paths with my one and only true soul mate," tone down tonight's goal to "meeting some nice new friends." If you don't come across a suave and sexy stranger you want to wed, you could still wind up meeting the link who will introduce you to the most important person in your life. Often the most successful people, with the happiest careers and marriages, are the ones who tried the hardest, fought the longest, and refused to give up until they got what they wanted.

Conduct Yourself Better on Blind Dates

"Valerie was right, you are beautiful" was the first sentence Aaron said to me on our blind date. "Good opener," I'd answered, thinking that was why I liked writers—they had the best lines. Aaron recalls that when I met him downstairs in the lobby of my apartment building, I was wearing tight jeans, black cowboy boots, a white T-shirt that showed off my tan, and a huge smile. That was in the fall of 1990, seventeen years ago. All of the couples I set up who are now married have distinct memories of the details of their original encounter with their mate. Initial impressions can stick forever.

So if someone has gone to all the trouble of hooking you up with somebody she thinks is special, please do your part and be on your best behavior. I know sometimes you're just not in the mood to dress up and be gregariously interesting and interested, or on display like a dancing monkey. You're preoccupied with work, or nervous, or already sure this blind date is going to be as dull as the last blind date you were on. Yet showing up an hour late, chain smoking, drinking too much, wearing ripped or dirty clothes, shoving seven rolls into your mouth before dinner, trashing your ex, spilling your entire psychosexual history, or propositioning your date after five minutes is not going to be seen as endearing. You might be turning off your date, as well as your matchmaker. Sometimes it's a lot of hard work to put two people together. It can require phone calls, e-mails, long conversations, descriptions, wading through many events, business cards, and friends of friends to come up with somebody who seems available, special, and appropriate. What fixer-upper wants to waste time and energy on a disrespectful clod who can't even be charming for half an hour?

Despite your mood, there is no justification for being rude or insensitive to a prospective date. Stop using the excuse that you were just being yourself. This is especially tiring if that self can come off as self-involved, self-sabotaging, or self-destructive and thus self-consciously single. Once, when a pal noted that I'd interrupted her several times in a row, I used the excuse that I was just being myself. She turned to me and said, "Yes, and perversely so."

The idea that it's cool to be completely natural, true, honest, and spontaneous, and "let it all hang out" is outdated and overrated, especially around people who aren't related to you. By not monitoring your clothes, words, speech, manners, hand gestures, eye contact, and overall disposition, and refusing to rein in your "real self," you run the risk of appearing arrogant, off-putting, troubled, tense, overbearing, and insufferable. Don't assume you know how you appear in public; most people don't have a clue. I certainly didn't.

Although I've been very comfortable speaking in front of large classes and lecture halls for decades, I was shocked to see myself on television interviews. Who was that fast-talking, neurotic woman who interrupted her host and couldn't sit still, her eyes darting around and her hands flying all over the place? For later appearances I hired a makeup artist and hairstylist, and asked a publicist or coach to come with me. I strongly suggest hiring someone to interview and tape you for an hour, or letting a friend or relative try, even with a camcorder. That way you can get a sense of how you might come off. If you're not pleased with your appearance and can afford it, consider a few sessions with a speech or acting coach, stylist, makeup artist, or personal shopper.

All of this might seem like an extravagant, time-consuming, and expensive experiment. Yet if there's a disconnect between who you think you are and how you seem to others, what other areas in your world is this affecting? It's bad enough if this is the reason why blind dates never call you for a second or third rendezvous. But what if it's why you didn't get that big job you really wanted? Or haven't been promoted at your current job for six years? Or why you were turned down by the co-op board? Or not invited to very many holiday parties this season?

I know it can be confusing when your old look, style, and "accept me for exactly who I am" attitude worked really well for you when you were a cute high school cheerleader or football player, a bubbly college student, or a serious graduate student quoting Camus. Yet when you're young and idealistic, people cut you a lot of slack. What was considered cute at fourteen, eighteen, and twenty-four can be downright grotesque at forty-four. Picture how silly someone might look still wearing the haircut and clothes she wore twenty years earlier. I recently watched a TV special where actresses from *Dynasty*, *Dallas*, and *Knots Landing* trashed the garish outfits that were considered hot in the 1980s. As we get older, we have to keep revamping, remodeling, and updating ourselves—physically and emotionally. In middle age less is forgiven, and minor social misconceptions and missteps can seem magnified.

When I walked into a holiday soiree my friend Penelope was giving last December, she barked at me to put my coat and bags in the other room, said "introduce yourself around, I'm too busy with the food," and ignored my repeated attempts to let her know I'd brought her expensive champagne that needed to be refrigerated. Feeling dejected, I sat down on the couch next to a woman I'd never met before. She said her name was Hillary and asked me what was wrong. "Penelope just yelled at me. I think I'm going to leave," I confided, feeling like crying. (I had walked over in an excellent mood, and was usually a tough cookie. So if I was near tears, I guessed it wasn't my imagination.) Hillary—who turned out to be an old friend of Penelope's—said, "I know, she just insulted me too. She's a little psycho tonight." We consoled ourselves by acknowledging that Penelope had been going through a rough time after a breakup, was broke, and felt overly anxious about throwing this party, fearing that everything wouldn't go as she'd planned.

After she served the food, Penelope came over and acted very warm and friendly. It amazed me that she had absolutely no idea how hurt Hillary and I had felt, or how harsh and hostile she'd acted upon greeting her guests just twenty minutes before. Penelope was in her forties, had never been married, and had asked me to set her up. She had many stellar qualities—she was absolutely brilliant, an excellent cook, and quite kind and nurturing deep down. Yet I sensed she had unresolved anger and other issues that she first needed to work on before any tryst would take. I wasn't going to fix up someone who could alienate somebody in seconds without even realizing it.

I bring up this example because it's not an unusual occurrence. Many smart and acclaimed people I meet have no idea how rude and obnoxious they can come off. Perhaps the more brainy, acclaimed, rich, or attractive someone is, the less he worries about manners or toning down his interpersonal conduct. The gorgeous supermodel Naomi Campbell is said to live up to her diva label, Donald Trump is haughty as hell, and Pablo Picasso was famous for his petulance. The brilliant Nobel Prize–winning poet Joseph Brodsky could get away with chain-smoking unfiltered cigarettes and throwing them on the floor in classrooms, parties, or wherever he felt like it. Still, luminaries in these categories are never known for their stable personal relationships. Most humans disregard normal social etiquette and polite protocol at their own peril. It's hard to be an outspoken, lawless, rule-breaking rebel and maintain a good (first) marriage.

I rarely buy the vague reasons that solo players offer for their long-term unhappy single status, especially when it's smart, successful, and attractive people spouting the clichés.

"All the good ones are taken," "I'm just a little picky," "I haven't been lucky in love," "Men want young gorgeous models, not successful strong partners," and "Women only want rich men to support them" might be partly true in some cases. In others, they might be easy, tedious excuses used to avoid honest self-examination and making compromises and improvements. If all of these trite adages are correct, then how do millions of couples in this country wind up walking down the aisle every year? Are all those married people luckier, younger, richer, more beautiful, or better than you?

Sorry, but if you've been frustratingly single for ten, twenty, or thirty years and can't find a partner, it probably isn't about fate, luck, looks, sociological tendencies, or gender politics. It's much more likely that you haven't been ready for the real thing, and that your failure to connect involves your very idiosyncratic fears, self-deception, confusion, or lack of conscious understanding of your motives and missteps.

When you have doubts about how your manner and behavior are perceived, ask a close married comrade, a family member you trust, your therapist, or matchmaker for honest feedback and advice. Be willing to try such simple suggestions as making more eye contact and smiling without speaking; they could change your entire outlook as well as the reaction you get from others.

I know this because when it came to dating, I used to be an expert at ruining romantic rendezvous before they even began. I'll never forget the time almost two decades ago when my happily married therapist Patricia Gross suggested that I act more feminine and flirty for an upcoming blind dinner date. At the time I was proud to see myself as a smart, snide, loudmouthed feminist and rough-and-tumble big-city journalist. So Dr. Gross's suggestion that I "put on a flowered dress, smile more, be quiet, and ask the guy questions without talking about my work or politics" for our initial rendezvous shocked me. It made me want to scream, cry, then kill her.

"Are you insane? You want me to be a barefoot cute little waif to make this male I don't even know feel big?" I yelled in her face. "You want me to get a lobotomy?"

"Let me tell you how you acted on your last blind date," she calmly said. "You wore baggy black jeans, a big black sweater, cowboy boots, marched into the restaurant with your big black briefcase, dropped it on the table, and babbled about your work for more than an hour. Then you insisted on paying for dinner and almost arm-wrestled the guy for the check. That's why he never called you back," she told me. "And then you spent months complaining that you're single and lonely and nobody calls to ask you out anymore."

"Really?" I asked, hurt by her caricature. Yet at the same time I sensed that her portrayal of how I first came off to a new guy as a ballbuster was accurate. Until she held up a mirror to the way I tended to treat men I just met, I could not see it. I had wondered why that last guy, a good-looking doctor, had never asked me out again. I recalled that after our dinner, he quickly put me in a cab, as if he couldn't wait to get away from me fast enough. I had thought he wasn't physically attracted to me. I didn't realize all the barriers I had subconsciously put up.

"I was just being myself," I whined to Dr. Gross.

"That self was rude and pretty out of touch," she said, challenging me. "Would you dress and act like that on an interview for a high-level job you really wanted? Or taking oral exams to get your Ph.D.? Or in front of the co-op board of an apartment you wanted to buy?"

I shook my head no. In all of those scenarios I would have dressed classier, kept my mouth shut, and only responded when I was spoken to. I would have tried much harder to make a more poised and elegant first impression. Not because it is better for a female to be quiet, sweet, mild, and not threatening; but because it was a means to an end, and a more judicious stance might have landed me exactly what I wanted. Later, if I came across my new boss, professors, or neighbors, I could be more comfortable and speak more freely.

"As an experiment, why don't you try it once my way? Just for tonight?" Dr. Gross suggested.

That night, for my date with Andrew, a good-looking corporate lawyer a friend had set me up with, I did it Dr. Gross's way. I put on a flattering flowered peasant skirt with—gasp—pink in it. I wore a demure white top, heels, lipstick, sweet perfume. I switched my huge briefcase for a delicate purse. I did not share my left-wing opinions or the details of my day at work at all. I spent most of the night smiling and pretending I was gathering background data for a newspaper or magazine interview. I asked the attorney innocuous questions about himself, such as, "Where are you from?" "Where did you go to school?" "Do you have sisters and brothers?" "What are your favorite hobbies?" "Do you like to dance?" "What are your favorite movies?" "What kind of music do you like to listen to?"

To my surprise, Andrew kept smiling back and asking me questions about myself that had nothing to do with how I made a living. When he went to pay the check, I let him and thanked him. As we strolled home, he put his arm around me, kissed me at my door, and said he'd call me. He called me the next morning, to say what a nice time he'd had. Ultimately it didn't work out. But the difference in my two dates had a profound effect on my perspective and the way I acted on dates from then on.

A few years later, I modified Dr. Gross's suggestions for my first date with Aaron. I ditched the skirt because I wasn't as comfortable wearing dresses and skirts and hated being told that men preferred feminine attire. I decided that I was allowed to dress comfortably whenever I felt like it, Dr. Gross and her stupid rules be damned. As a concession, I exchanged my usual baggy black Levi's and overlarge black sweater for a fitted, low-cut white top and tight jeans. I also kept her silly suggestions for pink lipstick and sweet perfume, and lost my big, fat briefcase. Over dinner, I was consciously quieter and asked him lots of questions. Aaron definitely liked me enough to date me. Yet after an off-and-on six-year courtship, he wouldn't propose.

When I really felt like I was ready to get married, I told Aaron to forget it and stopped returning his calls. Then I went out and bought a sexy, short black dress and strappy high heels, and began dating others. On his tenth offer for dinner, I reluctantly agreed to see Aaron again, making sure to don the black mini. Not much later he came back with a diamond ring, which I partially credit to that tiny dress. (Men might be limited, but how limited are you if you want one yet can't indulge their desire for a little visual stimulation every once in a while?) Aaron still insists that I pull that flimsy frock out of the back of my closet, put it on, and let him take it off, each year for our anniversary.

Last week my friend Wanda was complaining that her male therapist had advised her to tone herself down on dates. Proud of her fierce, outrageous, funny personality, Wanda was grossly offended. She called a feminist girlfriend, who said, "Fire the sexist bastard." When Wanda repeated the details to me, I guessed that her militant girlfriend was unmarried and single. (Surprise—she was.) I reassured Wanda that my female therapist had once given me the same advice. It had nothing at all to do with gender politics or value judgments. Indeed, what could be better for women's rights than a woman achieving her goals and getting exactly what she wants for herself? Meanwhile, I adored my husband and my career, while still being proud to call myself by the F-word.

By toning yourself down for dates, nobody is suggesting that you repress, alter, or transform your real self forever. The idea is to make a nice, nonthreatening, kind, easygoing, sane, stable first impression. You don't really want to scare, alienate, or offend somebody before you have time to even figure out if this person has potential, do you? Furthermore, regulating or reining yourself in is good advice for both men and women. Single men can also greatly benefit from toning down or adjusting their personalities to better charm and get to know potential partners.

Again, job hunting is a helpful metaphor to consider. Most professional males I know would never show up to a work interview unshaven, in ratty jeans, a torn shirt, or old sneakers. They would never drink too much, chain-smoke, show off, interrupt, or give too much information about their ex-wife's addictions or infidelity. Yet somehow on a date—or at a party or singles event—certain guys justify this kind of boorish behavior. Big mistake, because a blind date could be the most important interview of your life.

The best job I ever had lasted four years. So far my marriage to Aaron has lasted more than ten years and I hope it will endure forever. A healthy mate will support you in more ways than any employment ever could. You will be trusting your spouse with your body, soul, dreams, living space, and finances, and possibly raising your children.

Hal, an actor I dated, initially took me out to chic bistros, and always insisted on paying the check. I later found out that he was broke and going through a rough time with work. When I complained to Dr. Gross, she said Hal's instinct to suavely wine and dine me—even though he was really in debt and turmoil—was appropriate and smart. First dates are not the time to spill one's financial or career problems. She also reminded me that I often ran away from guys who too quickly poured out sob stories of being dumped by bosses or exes, or of being mistreated in their childhoods. Too much vulnerability too fast made them seem wimpy and turned me off. A strong male presence was more exciting. After I got to know the guy, I was more interested in learning all of his dimensions. I wound up dating Hal for six months and we are still close friends.

"But isn't it a lie to pretend you're someone you're not?" I challenged Dr. Gross.

"There's a difference between lying and showing restraint. If spilling every single fact about yourself too soon is the way you sabotage relationships because you're too scared of intimacy, isn't that more deceptive?"

"Isn't it phony to pretend I'm mysterious or play the hard-to-get game?"

"Not really," she said. "If your motivation is to sincerely get close to someone and certain actions or techniques work, then it seems honest to me."

I thought of that conversation recently, when Aaron came home from work and asked if I wanted to hear all about his horrible day. I answered, "Not if you want to get laid tonight." I was joking—sort of. But I disagree with all the advisers and experts who say that you have to share everything with your partner, who should be your best friend. You can have a lot of best friends, relatives, mentors, teachers, and a good shrink with whom you can share your every negative and petty complaint, angry comment, and ugly thought. Since you only have one mate, it doesn't hurt to continue to monitor yourself a bit after marriage. A little mystery can go a long way in keeping your marriage hot and happy.

Break through Your Dating Defenses

Change is not easy, especially when it comes to working on your personal style, preconceived ideas, and long-held attitudes about how you conduct yourself with the opposite sex. When I suggest toning it down, reining it in, altering a regular routine, or acting unusually quiet on a first rendezvous, many singles get angry, defensive, and outraged. Here's my usual response.

STATEMENT	ARGUMENT
"That's just who I am."	"Who you also are is single and lonely at thirty-nine."
"I've always been like this."	"Which is why you keep getting the same results."
"I met my last boyfriend this way."	"Then why aren't you still with him?"
"This used to work all the time."	"When you were in your twenties."
"My ex loved my raunchy sense of humor."	"Your ex, the cheating alcoholic?"
"My ex-girlfriend loved my fart jokes."	"The ex now married to the district attorney?"
"My parents were like this too."	"You don't want to be your parents."
"I want to be loved for my true self."	"Then make your true self lovable."
"I want unconditional love."	"Then adopt an infant or a puppy."

"Why should I listen to you?"

"I'm happily married, you're miserably single."

"Change makes me uncomfortable."

"Change can be uncomfortable and healthy."

"All my old relationships started this way."

"All your old relationships ended badly."

"What if it's just fate?"

"What if it's just fear?"

Play the Numbers

Despite all your deep soul-searching, strategizing, and complicated personal philosophies of dating and mating, sometimes it just boils down to a numbers game. Almost everyone I know who is wonderfully wed had to go to a lot of awkward parties, meet multitudes of almosts and maybes, and weed through a lot of frogs before kissing a keeper. Even when I'm sure I'll be able to introduce someone to the perfect match, it is very rare when the first introduction I make leads to marriage. I certainly didn't fall for the first suitor my matchmaker had picked for me.

Sick of all the wrong men I used to fall for, Valerie had several terrific prospects in mind for me and I agreed to be open-minded and go out with all of them. Marc was a French doctor on the short, angry side. Loren was a playwright on the tall, skinny side. Both were gentlemen whom I treated gingerly. Aaron, the TV/film comedy writer I fell for, was Valerie's guess number three. When I learned that my editor Dina wanted to meet someone, I introduced her to four different guys before she fell for Ted. When I planned a singles-only soiree for my Midwest friend Karen

Sosnick, she promised to have a drink with every guy from the party who liked her. Jeff, who is now her husband and the father of her adorable baby son, was date number five. And these are the wildly successful stories.

My old schoolmate Janet Hill, the beautiful forty-two-year-old founder of Harlem Moon Books, recently joked to the *New York Times* "Style" section that her husband was "blind date no. 999." That might have been an exaggeration, but I wouldn't be surprised if she really went on a hundred blind dates before her wedding, where she answered the reverend's question with, "I *absolutely* will."

You should try never to overfocus on one romantic potential or one rendezvous. Nobody needs added pressure. Instead, get into the swing of going to social events several nights a week in general. Dating around is definitely the way to do it. Monogamy comes much later. That's the beauty of cultivating connections with as many matchmakers as you can. It's not like sending your unpublished essay or article pitch exclusively to one editor and having to wait to get a response. When you are looking for a mate, multiple submissions are allowed and encouraged. Most matchmakers know this. It's hardly ever a one-shot deal, especially if you're smart and leave all options open.

I think Aaron's divorced friend Chris is a terrific guy, and have tried to set him up with a few different women over the last three years. He dated a novelist from my writing workshop for a few months, but ultimately it didn't get serious. Another woman friend who was thirty decided that Chris, at forty-eight, was too old for her. Did I give up after two no-gos? No way! I recently tried to connect him with someone else. Why did I keep trying? Because Chris always acted like a sweet, caring person, and was a pleasure—both to his dates and to his dating coach: me.

How to Treat Your Matchmaker after a Mismatch

Aside from treating yourself and your blind date with kindness and class, there's another relationship you now need to nurture. When you find somebody who is nice enough to attempt to set you up, think of this person as a long-term confidante and be appreciative. Acting sweet after success is easy. How you act after a failure will show your true colors. Even if your blind date is a disaster, here's what I suggest:

- Try a quick e-mail or phone follow-up to your fixer-upper, offering something good first. Saying "We had our date. Terry was extremely smart, as you described him, though I don't think it's a love match. But thank you so much for thinking of me," within a week or two will be greatly appreciated.

- Relay positive information about your fix-up to your matchmaker if he or she was kind or generous, even if the person was not for you. "By the way, Terry generously treated me to a fabulous Italian dinner. I offered to pay my share but he refused to go dutch. Very nice gentleman," or "Sally made me a fabulous home-cooked meal, which was so kind of her," only makes everybody look and feel good and want to fix both of you up again.

- You can add gentle specifics about what went wrong, along with the thanks, as in, "Terry was so smart and sweet but I've got my heart set on somebody really tall, like me." A tactful critique will be appreciated; in fact, I might immediately think of somebody six inches taller to try you with. I may also learn something interesting.

After I set up my lesbian neighbor Nora with Lily, who was dressed-down, butch, and athletic like she was, Nora explained she actually went for her opposite. She introduced me to her ex, who, to my surprise, was petite, made-up, and downright frilly. So while straight singles usually sparked to partners who were similar to them, it turned out my gay friends frequently went for a contrast.

- If the person you were paired up with was rude, insane, inebriated, married, living with someone, blatantly lying, or hiding other secrets, it is appropriate to calmly pass on this information. If your date is trying to trick you, chances are he or she is also tricking your fixer-upper. In my case I might want to cross this person off my list and not put anybody else through the test or trauma. After you share the story, it would be nice to add something like, "I know you didn't know" or, "Thanks so much for caring and trying." Ask yourself how often someone in your world makes the effort to fix you up more than once and—sometimes after decades of your breakups—keeps caring and trying.

- If your date was a kind, interested person with good manners who treated you well, but one you nevertheless found overweight, not brilliant or good looking enough, with bad teeth or bad posture or bad shoes, it is okay to express this to the matchmaker. Yet perhaps add the caveat, "I know this sounds superficial, but . . ." This will let me know that you know how hard it is to find somebody kind and interested who has good manners and treats you well. Some things—like bad shoes, nerdy haircuts, and yellow teeth—might be fixable if a sensitive matchmaker finds a way to relay the information.

- When you're next invited to a party or event, it is fine to ask if your former blind date will also be invited. It is also fair to say, "I might not come because it could be a bit uncomfortable." But it's even fairer—to you, your matchmaker, and the blind date—to get over it. Especially if the reason it didn't work out was superficial or a lack of chemistry.

- Attempting to make a new friend or acquaintance out of the date, or at least being warm, would be nice and create cool karma. After it didn't work out, I stayed friendly with Jeff, Bill, and Rich, inviting them to events I hosted. I ended up introducing all three of them to their wives. Aaron and I didn't catch fire after our first encounter, but wound up in love on the second go-round.

After a Date Gone Wrong, Please Never:

- Call your matchmaker and scream, "How the hell could you possibly think I would like such a loser?" This will make you look like a loser.

- Harp on the fact that your blind date was too fat, short, bald, badly dressed, or not good looking enough, or had bad teeth. Say it once, then move on. Focusing on your date's physical imperfections will make you seem like a superficial idiot—especially if you aren't such a twenty-year-old, skinny Adonis yourself. What if your date turns out to be a relative, mentor, or a good friend of the matchmaker's? (Did you ask first, before sharing the insults?)

- Go around trashing the imperfections of this person to others in the same crowd. It's a small world and it could get back to your imperfect but nice date, or your well-intentioned matchmaker. Never mind that one person's beauty is another person's beast and vice versa. Everyone is entitled to an off night and different taste. Just keep your negative thoughts where they belong—in your notebook, in your therapy sessions, and in conversations with your best friend and matchmaker. Would you want the whole world to hear bad things a mean date said about you?

- Overreact. Even if your date was rude, insane, inebriated, married, living with someone, blatantly lying, or hiding other secrets, don't forget that it was only one evening, for Pete's sake. You didn't waste your life, or years, with the person. Give yourself—and your matchmaker—credit for trying and move on. If you were naive and impetuous enough to loan him or her money or jump into bed on the first meeting, don't blame your matchmaker for your inane indiscretion and thank goodness you've learned not to rush like that again.

- Warn your matchmaker that he or she is never allowed to invite this person to an event where you might be. It will be easier to just stop inviting *you* to places altogether.

- Yell, grab your coat, run out the door, or otherwise make a scene if you happen to bump into your blind date another time. Drama queens (and kings) are draining, and hurting someone's feelings a second time is a total karma killer.

7

CHANGING THE LOOK OF LOVE

After you have a drink with a new date whom you don't particularly feel like jumping into bed with, you tell the matchmaker, "Nice try, but no go," and the game is over, right? *Wrong!* This is just where it starts to get complex and interesting.

Your first step post–blind date is not to inform your matchmaker, your mother, your best friend, your ex-lover who is now sleeping with your ex–best friend, your recent date, or even yourself that you are sure this was not a love match. Unless the one you were set up with stood you up, got drunk, picked his nose in front of you, or stuck you with the check for lobster while talking on a cell phone for an hour, it is also not yet time to decide that you will never see this person again. That's what you used to do in the past— make quick decisions based on superficial impulses. If you do the same thing, you will get the same results: an empty bed and an empty heart.

It is now time to do something different and exciting.

Do not rush to make a rash decision or judgment. Slow down, chill out, and think about what just happened. After your blind date is over, schedule a date with yourself, your feelings, and your notebook. If this feels awkward, weird, silly, or uncomfortable—all the better. Great changes often feel strange just because they are unfamiliar.

There are many reasons to take the time out to do this. First, you have so many emotions swirling around the issue of dating, mating, and marriage that the immediate feelings you experience are not necessarily accurate or based on anything but fear, frustration, habit, and misguided fantasies. Yes, that's right—I am saying *do not trust your gut*. (Well, if you hear your date utter the words *heroin*, *jail*, or *polygamy* on a first date and want to run, trust that gut.) But do not trust the gut that says, "This person is very nice but not good looking or well dressed enough for me so I'll never see him again. I just have no luck in love. Boo-hoo, poor me, case closed." Get that case reopened right away!

I know you are about to get defensive and paranoid that I'm trying to ruin your life by pushing you toward someone ugly, uncool, desperate, or otherwise totally not right for you. I'm not—I'm just trying to get you to reconsider the ridiculous rules and preconceptions that have been etched in your stubborn brain since junior high school. Remember, until now, your methods didn't work, which is why you are still single and complaining that you are companionless and lonely. All of the guys I ever felt instantly attracted to turned out to be liars, cheaters, or leeches. And like most of my joyously married girlfriends, it took me quite a while to really see, fall for, and fully appreciate the right qualities in a husband.

When I first met Aaron, I was sure he was not my type. You know what? He wasn't. He was different from most of the other idiots I had wasted years on. Something different often feels confusing, frightening, sad, or weird, and makes you want to run away. You can run away—just not yet. You first have to figure out exactly why you want to run away. It could be because this date is a bad person. Or because this date is a good person who is completely wrong for you, in which case you don't ever have to see him or her again.

Yet there's also a chance that this new person you just met might actually be available to love and marry you. Despite your insistence that you really want to tie the knot and settle down, deep intimacy scares the hell out of you. So you defensively find flaws, failures, and blemishes in your date, ruining the chance of any relationship instead of first confronting yourself to unravel what is really going on.

Now take out your notebook and, in the left-hand column, write a list of every nice, good, positive thing that could possibly be said about the person with whom you just went out on a date. Even if you didn't really like how he or she dressed or spoke or smiled, pretend that someone else is evaluating your student, child, brother, sister, or best friend, and be gracious, humble, unassuming, and generous. Give your companion credit for being well groomed, friendly, on time, cheerful, bright, engaging, interesting, interested, talkative, honest, sincere, open-minded, listening, and for asking questions. (Kind of like the qualities you'd look for in a personal assistant, business partner, or friend.) In the right-hand column, list everything negative, bad, off base, creepy, or annoying. Whether or not there's an initial attraction should be noted, but put into context and not given more credit than other qualities.

I know multitudes of singletons who are sure that immediate chemistry is the ultimate test, and that couples should click right away and feel instant attraction. You've seen this scene in the movies, the ones where the bells go off, firecrackers sizzle, the sky changes color, the outside world becomes mute at the mere sight of one's beloved. If you fit into the crowded category that believes this actually will happen to you, please lose this cliché right now. It is wrongheaded, off-base, dumb, silly, impatient, immature, shortsighted, and probably the most common reason why you are single and sitting alone in your house, watching these fake old flicks in the first place, bemoaning your solo status. But it isn't fate that's keeping you from getting what you want. It's you, and the fact that you are holding on to one of the most outmoded misconceptions available to woman- and mankind. In all other areas we give ourselves room to breathe and develop slow and steady connections. Yet when it comes to romance, everyone expects magic in half an hour.

Let's do some slo-mo analysis here. Think back. Did you click with every single close friend of yours from the second you first met? No. In fact, I bet you are currently hanging out with someone you initially couldn't stand. Did you take to every job you ever had from your starting day? Hell no! I'd guess there were a few positions where it took you weeks, months, or even years to adapt, get promoted, and hit your stride. (It took me two decades of hard work, self-questioning, and reinvention to land the career I desired. And I'm still working on it.)

Furthermore, was every single pet you adored in your life perfect, affectionate, and well behaved from the second you brought it home? Of course not. You invested time and money in training, teaching, and experimentation until you and your cat, dog, bird, snake, or hamster found mutually satisfying rules, rapport, and comfort. Now what about your family members? Did you always cherish your parents, grandparents, siblings, cousins, and extended clan? I would guess that it took you time to be able to understand, relate to, and appreciate certain relatives you currently feel a deep bond with. Did you ever move into the ideal apartment with the ideal decorations already in every single room? What a joke! Most of us painted, wallpapered, refurnished, redecorated, renovated, and/or did major construction before we felt our home was perfect for us. And we're nowhere near finished with the project.

There are many reasons you shouldn't judge someone instantly, or be swayed too much by visuals. Sometimes it will make you miss the bigger picture. I remember getting a free press pass to attend a PEN American Center conference on Eastern European nationalism in the 1980s, featuring the internationally acclaimed poets Joseph Brodsky and Czeslaw Milosz, whom I was supposed to interview. When I took note of the sophisticated, well-dressed crowd at the event, I felt underdressed and out of place in my black jeans and sweater. Especially when I heard a group of wealthy-looking women in designer suits making fun of two shabbily dressed old guys in the corner. One woman said, "Who let the homeless guys in?" I looked over and noticed that one man hadn't shaved, his hair was in his eyes, and he had a hole in the elbow of his blazer. The other fellow was wearing cheap rubber shoes and a funny cap. Upon closer inspection, I realized the two shabbily dressed guys in question were Brodsky and Milosz—the Nobel Prize–winning poets, professors, political heroes, and highbrow guest stars that the idiotic (albeit glossy-looking) women had paid to see.

I greeted Brodsky (whom I'd studied with at NYU) and he introduced me to Milosz. I pulled out my notebook and admitted that I needed a clear definition of "Eastern European nationalism," since I didn't really understand what the term referred to. I feared these intellectual giants would ridicule my lack of knowledge. Instead they joked they didn't know what it was either and intended to fake it with stand-up comedy. Like every literary-minded female who came into their orbit, I was soon under their spell. Hearing them speak for an hour was transformational. Their brilliance, humor, humility, and humanity made them more gorgeous than Brad Pitt and Leonardo DiCaprio. Not surprisingly, they both already had lovely, devoted companions (and apparently a flock of groupies following them everywhere they went).

Another reason to keep an open mind is that standards of beauty change constantly. One day curvy women like J-Lo, Beyoncé, and Queen Latifah are in; the next day all celebs appear blond and scrawny like Paris Hilton and Nicole Richie. Tastes and styles are subjective and the critical masses are fickle. Plus people can look different every night. Hairstyles, makeup, clothes, hats, glasses, shaving beards and mustaches, waxing unwanted hair, wearing heels, having a tan, feeling ill, taking medications, and sometimes even moods and the weather can alter someone's entire presentation. Looking over a contact sheet from a recent photo shoot, I found that my face was stunningly different based on each angle, lens, distance, flash, and with each kind of makeup, hairstyle, and specific outfit's shape and color.

Changing your appearance can be important and useful in certain situations—for example, getting a job in a different field, using a specific image to sell a product, or initially attracting someone of the opposite sex. (Unfortunately, many singles seem to base whom they will date mainly on looks.) Once, cohosting a singles party with a girlfriend, I came over early to find her wearing plaid culottes, a baggy white T-shirt, a ponytail, and no makeup. Since the purpose of the party was for her to meet available men, and she wasn't aware that she looked dowdy, I went to her closet and found a very flattering low-cut dress and high heels I suggested she try. I put her hair down and applied red lipstick and mascara. In ten minutes she looked like an alluring vamp and a completely different person. Four men asked her out that night, including the one she married, who is the father of her two children. I guessed he wouldn't have been as initially intrigued by her golf girl look.

To gauge by the current pop culture makeover craze, many people are willing to work on their externals, whether that involves a new wardrobe, hair dye, contact lenses, exercise routines, or plastic surgery. Although of course you should never say to someone, "I'll go out with you if you get a nose and chin job," you do have a little leeway with looks—even from the starting gate.

My friend Debbie was asked out repeatedly by Peter, a doctor she liked enormously as a person. But Debbie was slender and loved to exercise and Peter was overweight and out of shape. She discussed with her therapist Dr. Lee what a shame it was to give up on such a good-hearted, smart man. Dr. Lee advised her not to throw in the towel just yet. Instead, she instructed Debbie to nicely tell Peter the truth and see how he reacted. So when he next asked her out, Debbie let Peter know that working out was a big part of her life that she needed to share with a partner. Debbie found the conversation awkward, and he stopped calling her. She feared she'd hurt his feelings. But two months later Peter showed up at her office, twenty pounds thinner, and asked her to a play. They began dating. When he couldn't take her out to dinner because he was too busy doing his nightly workout routine at his new gym, she joined the gym too. Peter still has thirty pounds to lose, and it's too early to tell what the future will bring. I'm not suggesting everyone try this—obviously there are times when commenting on someone's weight could be mean, hurtful, or inappropriate. On the other hand, maybe it's worth it to find out if someone who is otherwise great would be willing to make dietary and exercise changes. The fact that Peter was willing to hear and understand what was important to Debbie showed her that he could have serious potential.

Plus, the fantastic news is, as you get to know, like, and trust someone, this person really does become much better looking to you. Inner warmth, kindness, and generosity have a way of melting your heart and altering your focus and perception. Instead of a stranger with faults that are easy to criticize, the one you are dating can easily become the bearer of warmth, sweetness, joy, and good tidings. Someone who appreciates you, dotes on you, and is able to express fondness and love can become more desirable by the minute. (Especially when you're sick of incapable jerks who treat you badly.) When you're truly ready for the real deal, somebody who treats you like royalty will gain in stature and beauty, and will look more regal in your eyes.

Physical attributes ultimately have little to do with how sexually turned on and satisfied one gets. The brain controls our climaxes more than our eyes. We've all once been with that gorgeous lover who wound up revealing selfishness, stupidity, vapidness, neediness, meanness, sickness, or superficiality to such an extreme degree that you bolted from the bed, rushed out the door, and never returned. Conversely, a bedmate of average looks who is sweet, funny, puts you at ease, and cares deeply about your sexual satisfaction is usually the best lover. People whose faces and figures are not so commanding often try harder to develop other skills to compensate, and you know what? It works!

A sudden turn in success can also spin your head around and make you bewitched, bothered, and bewildered. I began dating Aaron when he was a cute, albeit rumpled, freelancer. But when he became a staff writer on *Seinfeld*, I was impressed, turned on, and yes—I felt more attracted to him. Somehow his baggy jeans and untied sneakers now seemed more hip than shleppy, his shoulders appeared bigger, and his every word seemed smarter. While at his new job, Aaron admitted feeling more attracted to me too, and more "worthy" of love. (Hey, success, fame, and fortune are aphrodisiacs. That's why so many short, bald, funny-looking moguls are married to tall, gorgeous models.)

I did later realize that by being so awed by my suitor's TV job, I had merely traded one form of vanity for another. Yet if you have to be a snob, picking a partner for their stellar sense of humor and brains is more intrinsic to who that person is and thus a much better bet than marrying for their money or body. Meanwhile, when Aaron lost the great gig, became broke, and started freelancing again, I still loved him. Even so, we were off-and-on for a few more years before we finally figured out how to love, take care of, and enhance each other.

Yes, we all hear these love-at-first-sight stories. Usually they come from couples who met when they were teenagers. Or from some rich, male CEO discussing how he met his third or fourth wife (young enough to be his daughter) and, more often than not, while he was still legally married to his previous spouse. Or from starstruck celebrities, whose marriages last between three months and three years. Or from someone who rewrote the facts to sound more romantic to celebrate a silver or gold wedding anniversary.

It's understandable why pairs lie and pretend they took to their mate in minutes. They are afraid, ashamed, or too discreet to tell you the unvarnished truth because it can be ugly, superficial, unspectacular, or downright tacky. How would it sound if a longtime wife, mother, and grandmother told you: "I wasn't sure if he was smart enough for me. But I had to escape my religious family and he had a good-paying job, so I said 'What the hell' and gave it a shot." Or if a seventy-year-old father and grandfather admitted: "I'd just gotten out of the war. She had a big mouth and an overbearing mother, but I hadn't seen a woman in three years, her luscious breasts made me crazy, and she wouldn't do it without a ring on her finger, so what the hay?" Instead they smile and say, "It was love at first sight" and everybody oohs and aahs at their sweet proclamations of long-ago instant passion.

My theory is that once people go to all the expense and trouble of getting hitched, having kids, and wind up growing old together, they forget what they didn't initially like about each other. Or they've molded their partners so they're now better suited for each other. Or in order to encourage their children to wed and bring forth grandchildren, they gloss over the gory parts. Or they smartly focus on the wonderful romantic side and consciously block out flaws and failures.

People who actually pair off passionately right away run the risk of burning out quickly. When you start with amazingly high expectations that *this is the one*, you usually have nowhere to go but down. If, on your first meeting, you think someone is gorgeous and perfect, what happens when you see your date the second time? How can anyone keep up with that ideal image? What if this person wears the wrong outfit? Or gets a pimple? Or a bad haircut? Or a cold? What if he has a learning disability? Or she has a troubled family? Are you leaving your dream mate room to be human? What do you actually know about the individual whose arms or bed you just jumped into based on oval-shaped eyes, overwhelming charm, or impressive physique? Unfortunately, sometimes the look of true love and true lunacy can overlap.

I once had fairy-tale first and second dates with a tall, handsome, well-built teacher who seemed so taken with me that his excitement was intoxicating. On our third date, I noticed a mark on his wrist and asked about it. He confided that he'd been diagnosed as schizophrenic, had tried to kill himself twice before, and was currently on antipsychotic medication. Although learning that someone was taking medicine for a psychiatric problem wasn't necessarily a deal breaker for me, it was motivation to gather more personal data about him. When I did, he admitted that his doctor did not think he was in good enough shape to get seriously involved with anybody at the moment. I was glad that I found all this out before I slept with him, and relieved that I hadn't been too blinded by his great looks to ask important questions.

My girlfriend Wanda recently told me a similar story about a whirlwind courtship she'd had with a new adorable hunky guy. He'd taken her out for two amazing dates two nights in a row. Then he'd sent flowers and called her four times the next day to say how much fun he'd had. No games, no waiting. She couldn't believe her good fortune—until his soaring energy crashed by the end of the week and he canceled their plans because he couldn't get out of bed. He admitted that he was bipolar and seeing a doctor to try to control the intense daily highs and lows. They ended up friends. But she wound up feeling disappointed and angry with herself for getting way too excited too quickly.

I am in no way saying that you should rule out anyone who is being treated for an illness. But often *when something seems too good to be true, it is.* Think Ted Bundy. Because the serial killer was so good-looking, many innocent women attributed good, honest qualities to him that he didn't have—to their peril. Con men and women, criminals, adulterers, drug addicts, liars, alcoholics, and serial cheaters can be very convincing. If you're too susceptible to instant allure, they could reel you in. Some people who are schizophrenic, sociopathic, hypomanic, and manic depressive actually believe what they are saying when they say it, so it's hard to tell if they are lying.

I recently heard the novelist Terry McMillan tell Oprah how heartbroken she was when the younger man she married and wrote about in *How Stella Got Her Groove Back* turned out to be gay. They'd first met on a Caribbean vacation. The psychologist on the show nodded when McMillan spoke of the fantasy fling they'd had on a tropical island. But she asked the author what had compelled her to take her young fantasy fling home. She wasn't assigning blame. But the fascinating psychological question was: what need or hole in this extremely successful and intelligent woman's life was so immense that it had caused her to turn off her brain and miss all the signals?

In other words: don't just fling yourself at someone young, buff, or fabulous looking as fast as you can. Your goal is to find a serious, healthy, appropriate partner to be your closest family member for the next twenty, fifty, or sixty years. Slow down and make sure that what you see is really what you'll be getting.

Take time to ponder the down and dangerous side to letting someone's luscious face, hot body, or huge bank account loom too large in your decision-making process. As they age people can lose their looks—and their earning potential. So what happens after you triumphantly strut down the aisle with your rich and gorgeous, svelte hunk of burning love? If he or she gains weight, loses too much weight, gets bad skin, goes bald, winds up with wrinkles and cellulite, or makes a bad financial investment and forfeits the family fortune, is it all over? Do you then divorce, feeling like you've been tricked out of what was promised? You will be safer and better off in the long run if you slow down and ponder what are really essential qualities to find in a spouse. A beautiful shell that hides a bad person equals zero. Honesty, kindness, and integrity need to be at the top of your list, before sex appeal and earning potential.

When my girlfriend Annie, a florist in her late thirties, met Steve, a sweet, hardworking younger guy, she wasn't sure he was her type. In the past, she would choose a guy based on his clothes and external style, how he wore his hair, if he had a cool profession or sophisticated manner. Steve, on the other hand, was warm, real, and chatty, with a goofy sense of humor. He was very close to his family and not afraid to be emotional and uncool at times. Annie decided he was her new type, and they married. They were then hit with a series of calamities, including miscarriages, infertility, unemployment, a difficult adoption, and a serious illness that could have been fatal. All the traumas convinced Annie that she had indeed picked the right partner, for all the right traits. "When I was in my twenties, I went for all the wrong qualities in men," she told me. "Now I know that the most important question to ask is: if I'm sick, will he come to the hospital to see me every day and bring me flowers?"

8

HOW TO RECOGNIZE
GOOD RAW MATERIAL

My husband hates when I even imply that we weren't 100 percent sure of each other from the first date forward. But I like to come clean about our initial hesitations, because this is where many smart people get hung up. At a recent singles party I gave, Phyllis, a good-looking guest who came with a friend, saw Aaron and me holding hands and looking at each other adoringly, and asked me, "How did you get so lucky?" Focusing on surface sheen, she acted as if this perfect specimen had just fallen from the sky right in front of me and handed me a diamond ring. Yet the handsome, well-groomed, wildly successful, adoring man, with whom I was completely in tune and harmoniously cohabitating in an elegant apartment, was not whom I met on our first date. That guy had some good qualities, but he was heavier, less well groomed, less social, angrier, less employed, in debt, living in a cluttered studio apartment, and nowhere near as chivalrous, in touch, or understanding of my needs and idiosyncrasies as he is now.

He would say the same of me. In fact, he detested that I smoked, drank, partied, wore torn jeans and sweatpants almost every day, and hated wearing skirts and dresses. He poked fun at me for being overly concerned with my diet and exercise, and used to warn: "I could never live with someone who only has diet soda and yogurt in their refrigerator." He accused me of being so busy playing the role of feminist and proving how tough I was that I was often cold and insensitive to his needs.

At the same time, Aaron and I both saw that we had decent raw material to work with. We were impressed with each other's heart, brain, soul, strength, and sense of humor. We were both honest, sincere, and hardworking, from tightly knit families we are still close to. Compared to solid, essential attributes like *impressive moral fiber, capable of deep, long-lasting friendships*, and *inherent emotional generosity*, the imperfections (like my smoking habit and big mouth, or his pizza habit, untucked shirts, and untied sneakers) appeared smaller. We learned to listen, argue, negotiate, compromise, refocus, quit bad habits, pick up better habits, and listen some more, working hard on our relationship for thirteen years. We had to become more successful separately before falling deeply in love and in sync.

Initial impressions aren't always accurate, and it often takes time to really get to know who someone is inside. Still, there are basic ways to figure out whether a person you meet is worthy of more attention. Try to put aside how good looking, sexy, or rich somebody is, and start by asking yourself these simple questions:

Does our matchmaker or mutual friend say my date is a good person?

Does my date seem like a good person to me?

Does she seem like an honest person?

Did he call and show up as agreed?

Does this person appear to be kind and friendly?

Do we have small things in common?

Do we share any common values?

Does this person like his or her city, home, friends, and job?

Does this person have a plan for life that sounds interesting?

Does the person seem comfortable in his or her own skin?

Would he or she treat my family and closest friends well?

Would my family and closest friends like this person?

Why would my family and closest friends like this person?

Does he or she seem interesting and interested in me?

Does this person make me laugh?

Does this person make me feel comfortable and safe?

Does this person say nice things about his or her family, pals, and exes?

Would it be nice to see this person again?

Can this person teach me anything I don't know?

Is this somebody I could trust?

The night of that singles party, Phyllis came around later to ask if I'd fix her up. She was a slim, pretty, thirty-six-year-old woman who'd never been married who heard about my reputation for matchmaking. Instead of asking me questions about my methods, or wanting to listen to advice about how I found my partner, she immediately listed the top qualities she wanted in a mate: great looks, height, success, money, class, a good career, great apartment, and a slim, athletic build. She asked, "Does your husband have any brothers or friends just like him?"

I was sure that if she'd known Aaron when I had first met him, she wouldn't have given him the time of day. Though he is great looking, he didn't have "a slim, athletic build" at the time, nor did he have a luxurious apartment or big bank account. In fact, when I'd originally asked him what he did, he'd said, "I'm currently broke and unemployed." When I asked, "What did you do when you were employed?" he mumbled, "Freelance writer." It was only after I'd begged to read his work that I learned he was incredibly brilliant and had a hysterically funny, self-deprecating wit. The fact that he was understated and the opposite of a show-off or a name-dropper made him even more special and appealing. Like most truly talented artists and writers, he wasn't overly polished and didn't sell himself well. So searching blindly for an obvious Prince Charming, Phyllis might have dismissed Aaron without asking the most important aforementioned questions or tuning in to what made him so rare and amazing. She could have completely overlooked or missed all of his subtle gifts and vast hidden potential.

At first I was taken by Phyllis's beauty. But she became less beautiful as she went on and on about her elaborate, trite romantic reveries while ignoring the twenty available, nice, healthy, local, bright, interesting single men I had invited to my home that night. I tried to introduce her around, but she let me know that none of the guys were her physical type. Okay, on a quick glance, some of the dudes in my living room might be labeled nerdy, not dressed in designer clothes, balding, on the short side, broke, unemployed, underemployed, in between jobs, afraid to commit, overweight or too skinny, too old for her, too young for her, too needy for her, too shy, or a bit too blustery.

But so what? Instead of talking to all of them to see who was smart, sweet, or interesting, Phyllis wasted an hour reciting all the superficial traits in her ideal man to a married host, who started to see her as superficial. Many single males and females like Phyllis regard being set up with an imperfect companion for one evening as an insult, or even fraternizing with the enemy. They act like they are doing their matchmaker—or their potential date—a big favor by even considering such an offer. They hide behind the mantra "I won't settle," while they actually wind up settling for half a life. Not because they don't have spouses or children, but because they don't have emotional insight or the guts to dig deeper into their dislike of any human flaws. I wish people like this could see the distortion in their logic and view the larger issues. The person who would profit most from Phyllis getting over her small-minded mentality would be Phyllis herself. Sharing love with a warm, kind human being often makes you smarter, safer, warmer, and a pleasure to be around—regardless of your mate's looks, height, profession, attire, jewelry, bank account, or the square footage of any real estate holdings.

The benefits of learning how to share, compromise, and connect with a truly committed mate are endless. So are the perks. Studies show that happily married couples are literally more successful, protected, and taken care of. They have higher incomes, better insurance and health coverage, and longer life spans—and so do their children.

If I'm asked to perform a fix-up, I ask questions and try to carefully delineate between someone who is a true sufferer of bad fortune versus one who is the architect of his or her own misery. I can completely empathize with a widower who can't re-create the magic he had with his late love. I also feel for divorcées, especially if they have to raise children alone. Before I married, I endured several breakups that felt like death, and

I automatically sympathize with anyone who was dumped by someone they loved. Once, twice, even four or five times (as I was).

But a solitary person who has done his share of dumping and has been complaining for decades that he can't find a mate, while relaying his every long horrible relationship war story, risks coming off as exhausting, draining, alienating, and toxic. Especially if all of the sexual sagas—and mistakes—keep following the same trite pattern. Usually it involves the pursuit of married, unavailable, rich, famous, or beautiful partners, along with the inability to feel attraction for someone nice on their level. More often than not, the enraged, heartbroken party is not open to new suggestions, such as: Join a new gym or sports team. Volunteer at a local soup kitchen or hospital. Pursue a different career. Get an unusual degree. Call a therapist. Attempt to be open to someone good, honest, and strong who might not come in your fantasy package.

The ultimate advantage of marriage is that you get to live according to the buddy system, with a guardian angel always covering your back. If you're sick, needy, hungry, horny, unemployed, lonely, in trouble with the law, or going crazy, you turn to your mate—whose job it is to bail you out, feed you, love you, take care of you, and vice versa. I was broke and on my own for fifteen years in the Big Apple, and many of my closest friends are still living solo. So I know how difficult it is to be a nonconformist in a world that seems made for conservative married couples with kids. I admire freelancers, freethinkers, aspiring artists, and individualists determined to be different. I find people who are having adventurous, career-filled lives on their own to be exciting, worthy of seeking out socially and supporting in every way imaginable.

I often treat single, financially strapped pals to meals and tickets to events, loan money when it's needed, offer to accompany friends to the hospital or doctor's office, include extra guests for holidays that can be depressing, like Thanksgiving and New Year's, and hang out until three in the morning when I sense someone is lonely, needs human interaction, or feels bad that they don't have anybody to go home to. I understand when our single friends crave companionship and invite Aaron to go out on Saturday nights, Sunday afternoons, and on vacations without me. He understands when I'm out for six-hour stretches because I'm paying an emergency house call to someone hurt and freaking out over a bad breakup.

What gets frustrating is listening to somebody on their own who is resentful, angry, and negative about relationships, while remaining close-minded. In most cases I don't buy the implication that one's single status is the fault of cruel sexism or the mean unfair world, and is thus impossible to work on or change in any way. It's hard to see the good-looking, smart, educated, employed, healthy, capable individuals I know as the poor helpless victims they can sometimes make themselves out to be.

I met a pretty, wealthy, forty-three-year-old woman who bemoaned being unmarried but refused to go out with a guy if she didn't like his shoes. A handsome, successful, forty-seven-year-old male friend of mine is continually cursing the twenty- and thirty-year-old beauties he asks out because they don't understand or appreciate him. Yet he won't even try a normal-looking woman his own age. These two like to see themselves as lone, brave soldiers unwilling to compromise, holding out for their noble aspirations of matrimony. Maybe they are. Or maybe she should get over her passion for $300 Gucci loafers, and it's time for him to buy dinner for a woman over thirty-five who wears size ten.

Their issues sound silly until you carefully investigate your own fetish for finding someone with the perfect pedigree, religion, background, age, weight, hair, height, home, finances, car, or career. Often if you could just get over one of your pre-occupations, you would have thousands more chances for success. At a certain point you have to stop blaming fate when it's really your unexamined vanity, superficiality, or unconscious fears that's screwing you out of love.

Someone continually incapable of maintaining a long-term intimate connection with another human being can be emotionally limited, with unmet needs he unrealistically expects relatives, colleagues, and friends to fill. Being extremely picky, with idiosyncratic lists of your ideal mate, might seem typical or cute when you're young. But growing old alone ain't pretty. Throw in a sudden career downturn, money problems, or illness and you've got the recipe for disaster. It's sad and aggravating when so often getting it together involves only intelligent compromise and accepting the affection of the ones who like and want to be with you. There's nothing wrong with your fantasy of marrying a gorgeous, rich, famous, fabulous movie star. But when that doesn't happen, you can learn to get over it, grow up, and move on.

While chasing after the Cinderella-like illusion that a fault-less fellow would walk through the door and save her, my guest Phyllis missed the chance to interact with real people. She wrongly felt that she was better off alone than with someone who wasn't handsome, tall, or successful enough. (Why? Was she that insecure with her looks or career that she needed wealthy arm candy to validate her?) She mistakenly assumed that landing true love was fast and easy for me and other women she was just meeting. And that a fantastic spouse comes polished to perfection, ready-made and wrapped in a ribbon.

I struggled with self-image, had my heart slaughtered several times, and I went to therapy to wrestle with my demons. Then I changed, conceded, argued, submitted, confronted my narcissism and unrealistic expectations, settled, made decisions I didn't quite feel ready for, and ultimately struck a balance—as did every other married person I ever met. Perhaps we were lucky, but the harder you work, the luckier you get.

My own list of my first date with my husband would have looked like this:

GOOD QUALITIES	BAD QUALITIES
Cute with nice, long, curly hair	Shleppy dresser, untied laces on his sneakers
Really tall, I could wear heels	Overweight, ate fried food
Clearly found me attractive	Called people who work out "mindless"
Didn't seem to mind my smoking	Didn't smoke or drink, seemed too straight
Seemed smart	Seemed too old for me and too conservative
Cool writing career I could relate to	Freelancer, no steady job
Funny sense of humor	Seemed sarcastic and angry at times
Asked about me and my work	Mentioned ex-girlfriend three times
Likes books, TV, plays I liked	Liked thrillers, mysteries, action flicks I hated
Treated for dinner	Made fun of me for ordering plain chicken
Was a gentleman	Was eleven years older than me, too old

Lived in and loved the same city as me	Lived in a tiny, messy place
Nicer than my old boyfriend	Not as buff and athletic as my old boyfriend
Asked me out again, no anxiety	Too eager, not mysterious

Now that I've scared you into thinking you will die friendless, pathetic, and alone, let's use that extreme perspective to review your good-bad blind date list. If any of the negatives you noted are such deal breakers as married, living with someone, bisexual, currently using drugs, deserted children, or mentioned liking threesomes, you can call it a day and move on to the next date or matchmaker. If that's not the case, but you really feel like you would throw up if you had to kiss the other person, you have permission to move on. If you're not sure, and there are more goods than bads, or the same amount of assets and liabilities, let your matchmaker know you would go out with the person again. When in doubt, seek suggestions from your fixer-upper, who might already know the other side's reaction and can advise accordingly.

As you can see in my case with Aaron, there were no extreme negatives that counted as deal breakers. I did kiss Aaron good-bye after our first dinner and it was nice. I could find many good things to say about the guy. Even though I felt no real explosive chemistry at first, was still hung up on the idiotic buff ex-boyfriend who was still calling me, and had several reasonable objections, I also felt like Aaron could be my pal or confidant. There was at least as much I liked about him as I didn't like. I can't tell you how many times I have thanked the Love Gods for my astute matchmaker who told me that I'd be crazy not to try with

Aaron again. It was the best decision I ever made, especially since the real explosive, exciting chemistry came later.

Fair Criteria for Turning Down a Second Date

- This person appeared to be married or living with someone. That he pursued me before splitting with his old partner indicated something negative about his character.

- This person said she had to stay in a bad relationship for the sake of the children, financial reasons, or because her long-term partner was sick or otherwise needy.

- She was cryptic when I asked for clarification of her marital status or living situation and didn't want to give me her home address or phone number.

- This person mentioned multiple marriages, divorces, separations, live-ins, and children. Since I'm single and childless the thought of all the people in his complicated past overwhelmed me.

- This person is currently living with his parents, his ex, his ex's family, or several roommates, which seems odd for someone over thirty.

- This person flirted with the waitstaff, the bartender, or a friend we bumped into.

- This date seemed to have no stable place to live, no stable job, or I sensed a shady past.

- This person name-dropped the famous friends she hangs out with or mentioned her fancy jet and Hamptons estate so often that she seemed way too insecure and show-offy. People who really have it don't need to flaunt it, right?

- The casual mention of current drug taking, alcoholism, gambling, financial debacles, or any other kind of illegal activity was worrisome.

- The allusion to untreated bipolar disease, schizophrenia, or a suicidal past seemed like a warning sign.

- This person trashed his ex, his mother, and his matchmaker—all on a first date! (How is he going to be talking about me next week?)

- This date was an hour late with no apology, spoke on his cell phone, left early, stuck me with the check, or was otherwise blatantly rude.

- I was so repelled by this person that the thought of kissing him nauseated me.

- She insulted, belittled, or kept interrupting me in a way that made me feel worse about myself.

- He proselytized about his religion, therapy, AA group, vegan-hood, or ideas about love, marriage, and children in an obtrusive way that seemed to leave no room for different styles or disagreements.

- He told me some long sob story about why he was currently broke, jobless, homeless, left at the altar, a victim of a scandal, or in a protracted legal battle, which made me feel like he desperately wanted to be saved.

- She asked me for money, drugs, a place to stay, a job, a recommendation, or to borrow my car on the first date—which is never a good sign.

- He asked me to meet his parents, children, ex-spouse, boss, or best friends on the first date, which is never a good sign either. Why the rush?

Dumb Criteria for Turning Down a Second Date

- Though he was decent looking, I didn't want to sleep with him immediately.
- This date didn't dress the right way or I didn't like the shoes he was wearing.
- My friends wouldn't find him or her cool.
- This person doesn't live in a nice enough neighborhood.
- This person doesn't make enough money or work in a field as cool as mine.
- This person might be smart, but she didn't go to as good a school as I did.
- I'm a true artist and this person is a suit with a boring office job.
- This date doesn't dig the same music, TV shows, movies, books, and magazines as I do.
- This person is not as good looking, buff, rich, famous, or funny as my last lover (who dumped me four years ago).
- This person might be cute and kind, but he was married before and I don't want to be someone's second or third spouse.
- This date has children from a previous marriage. Though it sounds like he or she is a good parent, I don't think I want children.
- This person has never been married at forty, so there must be something wrong with her.
- This person is not in good shape and I like to work out.

- Unlike me, this person smoked, had two drinks, or ordered meat, so it's already obvious we're not the least bit compatible.
- It seemed like he was trying too hard to be friendly and make conversation. If you have to work this hard, it's just not natural, you know?
- I didn't like the restaurant she chose.
- We didn't agree on all political issues that came up.
- He came from a family less successful and educated than mine.
- Though kind, thoughtful, and available, this person is ten years older (or younger) than me or lives in a different city or country now—so it can't possibly work out.
- We're from different ethnic or religious backgrounds, so it'll ultimately be too hard.

Decent Criteria for a Second Date

- Though not my type, this date seemed nice, kind, generous, and sweet.
- This date appeared to be making a big effort to be on time, dress nicely, be entertaining, and treat.
- I'm sick of sitting alone by myself, complaining about my single status, and this is the only offer for dinner I've had all month, or all year, so I'm going for it.
- I'm going to do something different this time, trust my matchmaker's opinion, and give this person one more shot, even if it doesn't feel easy or comfortable for me.
- He asked me many questions about myself and seemed warm and interested in my answers.
- Although we're in different fields, this date seemed very smart and hardworking.

- I liked the loving way he spoke about his parents, sibling, children, friends, colleagues, and pets.

- When talking about past relationships, she took part of the blame, admitting, "I was too immature back then, but I'm working on myself."

- This person shared her plan for how she was working to improve her education, job prospects, health, family life, apartment, or emotional situation in a way that sounded sincere.

- Even though he wasn't my type, it did feel nice and flattering to be treated so special.

- This date seemed like somebody I could see becoming friends with.

- Although I didn't feel overtly sexually attracted, the date was at least neutral and nice looking, and I was not repelled either.

- This person walked me home and waited until I was inside, or put me in a cab, in a way that felt protective or nurturing.

- The kiss at the end of the date was pleasant.

- His education, job, ambition, personal improvements, and the books he read impressed me.

- If this person lost weight, worked out, got a different haircut, or dressed better, I bet he'd be much cuter.

- This date seemed quite taken with me.

- This date seemed like a smart, rational, sturdy, honest, good, real person.

I know that it's much easier and more fun, entertaining, and seemingly cooler to maintain a cynical, bitter, distanced, postmodern, and ironic pose. I myself wore all black clothes and went around crying, "I am in mourning for my life" all through graduate school. This was while I was smoking, drinking, sleeping with Mr. Wrong, and wondering why nobody nice wanted to slip a diamond ring on my finger. I later learned that in order to have good luck with matchmakers, mating, and dating, you have to get rid of your selfish, self-involved, self-righteous, lazy impulses. Yes, it can be a real fight to find your optimistic, cheerful, healthy, nurturing, and self-validating side. But if you're ready to get married and stay married, there are rules of mundane social interaction that you should attempt to follow.

Nobody wants to date, court, or marry a close-minded, critical perfectionist who is going to judge, criticize, or rate him daily. Instead, the minute you meet someone new and nice, be conscious of how you're coming off and act kinder than usual this time. Learn how to lighten up, cut someone slack, forgive imperfections and limitations, and allow another person to be human. When you feel sarcasm coming on, hold your tongue. This patience and politeness will serve you well on date two, year two, or decade two.

For example, in the morning, when you can't see straight without your caffeine fix, if your lover asks you a question, you answer. If it's an obvious, angry, or stupid question, such as, "Where the hell are my gloves?" you try to refrain from snapping: "Wherever the hell you left them. What am I, your mother?" Instead I have learned to answer: "I don't know, honey, let me help you." Then I pat his hair, kiss his forehead, put down the newspaper I really want to finish reading, and search for his stupid glove until I find it on the radiator, exactly where he left it. Sometimes I add something flattering, albeit inane, like, "You're smart to wear your gloves today 'cause it's so cold outside."

Similarly, when Aaron comes home late at night, I greet

him sweetly. Even when I'm lying comfortably on the couch with a blanket over my legs, engrossed in a sexy movie on Lifetime TV. Okay, so I don't always feel like jumping up to kiss and hug him hello, cooing: "Hi, sweetie. I missed you. How was your day?" But I do it anyway. No matter how much I don't feel like it, I fake it. Why? Because the next evening, when I'm on a crying jag after an editor rejects my work, my husband—despite his mood or his bad day—will take me in his arms and say, "You're brilliant, and he's an idiot who I'm going to go beat up for you." We both try hard to come out of ourselves and our moods and to muster up good energy. By doing so, we make each other feel loved, cared for, safe, protected, and appreciated in our living space and marriage. In fact, that could be the definition of a perfect partnership: we both feel that it's our job to make each other as happy and comfortable in the world as possible. Sounds simplistic and corny. But after ten years of marriage, there's no place else we'd rather be than at home, in the haven of each other's arms.

Ways to Focus on the Positive

- After a blind date, jot down all the details in your notebook or journal. Even if it didn't go well, mark a star next to "survived blind date" and give yourself a lot of credit for trying.

- Write down every good thing about the date—even if it was just that you got to try a new restaurant, or wore a new outfit and felt comfortable, or felt less nervous than you expected to feel.

- Write down everything you did right—even if you weren't attracted and don't think you'll see the date again. Were you on time? Did you dress well? Did you ask questions and feign interest in subjects you don't know about? Did you learn something new about your date's field? Were you kind and open to this person?

- Write down every single nice thing you can think of about your date, even if you weren't attracted and don't think you'll see the person again. Was he the right age? The right height? Did the person show up on time? Dress nicely? Ask you questions? Try to impress you? Treat?

- If your date liked you more than you liked him or her, can you just focus for a minute on how nice it feels to be with someone who felt charmed and attracted to you? Isn't it so much better than the creepy feeling you had when a previous date was clearly not interested, faked a cell phone emergency, and left after half an hour?

- If it was a particularly negative or rejecting date, give yourself a present: a massage, manicure, pedicure, new haircut, new CD, a book, or a long long-distance call to a great friend you miss.

- If it was a particularly negative or rejecting date, do not have five drinks, smoke a joint, eat two pints of chocolate ice cream from the container, or call an ex who hurt you.

Reach Out and Touch the Right Someone

If you are confused, hurt, or anxious about what just happened on your blind date, the desire to pick up the phone is understandable. But if you can help it, try not to get on your cell on the cab ride home. Instead be quiet, think, let yourself feel how you feel, journal, and have a date with yourself first. If you must blab with somebody, there are several people *not to call now:*

- The date you just left.
- The ex you just broke up with.
- Someone single, bitter, or negative who is going to trash you or make you feel worse.
- Your matchmaker.

You thought the whole point of a matchmaker was to have someone to call and gossip with after your date, right? I'm not saying don't, I'm suggesting that maybe you should *wait* until you've had a little more downtime to figure things out and decide how you're going to respond. Why? Because if you're impulsive or impatient you might overreact and say very negative—or very positive—things too quickly that you could regret. Blurting out: "I'm completely in love with her! She's so gorgeous! I want to call her tonight and ask her out again! What did she say about me?" could be embarrassing, especially if you learn that your gorgeous date had already relayed that she was not interested or attracted to you at all. That means you might have missed signals or gotten a bit too gung-ho. Telling your matchmaker: "I hated his guts, he seemed preoccupied the whole time, very weird guy," could also be problematic. Especially if the date turned out to be the matchmaker's boss or close friend.

You could change your mind, or later learn more information that sways your opinion of what happened. For example, what if that quiet, preoccupied "weirdo" you had a drink with was on a new pain medication after knee surgery that spaced him out? Or he'd just lost his job and was having a hard time holding it together? Perhaps he didn't want to cancel last minute because he didn't want to be rude, or dump too much heavy stuff on somebody he just met. That would be smart and sensitive of him, no?

Would you feel differently about your date if you learned

that her husband had died of cancer ten months before? That was the case with Dana, a beautiful thirty-year-old woman friend I fixed up. It was a great sign that she felt ready for the small step of having a cup of coffee with somebody new. But she decided not to share the intensely tragic story of her widowhood yet, and asked me not to mention it. (She felt it might overwhelm somebody her age and wanted to give out the facts at her own speed.) That could be why she might have come off a bit aloof, weird, or self-protective.

If you must connect and confer with others right away, call, e-mail, or go see other good people: your mother, your favorite sibling, your therapist, or your closest friends—if these people were not your matchmaker. See what they say. Often if you ask the opinion of a few important people in your life, there will be a consensus. It's not that you are a baby who can't make a decision on your own. It's just that too often you've jumped headfirst into connections with people who are not worthy of you. You don't want to get hurt again, or misread situations, or waste more of your time. People you trust could be smarter, more detached, and thus more rational. The goal is to teach your brain to become the doorman to your heart. Doorman, not doormat. So you'll be able to rationally decide who is safe, who gets let in, and who is banned forever.

Make sure you mark in your notebook who fixed you up, the name of your date, where and when you went out, and what the relationship is between the date and the matchmaker. Regardless of whether you are going to see the potential match again, you should thank your matchmaker for thinking of you. You could send a card, a letter, an e-mail, leave a phone message, or tell her in person that you appreciate her efforts.

If your matchmaker says your match liked you and wants

to go out again, but you still feel unsure, you can now discuss it with your fixer-upper. But don't blurt out the first thing that comes into your head. It's best to start by saying something nice. "He was a real gentleman, though I'm not sure if it was meant to be," is a completely fair and classy comment. Listen carefully to the response. If your matchmaker immediately says, "I've got another guy for you," that might mean your date was not interested in seeing you again anyway. If your matchmaker says, "You really have to give him another shot," you might want to listen and let yourself be coerced. She could know things that you don't know—that he just got a huge job raise and promotion and is really going places. That he's so wild about you he'll do anything to win your love.

After my girlfriend Karen went out on a first date with Jeff, she called me and said, "He was nice." I said "nice" was very good, and suggested she give him another shot. Turns out Jeff had called his best friend and said, "This is the woman I am going to marry." And he did! Sometimes being loved and appreciated can be an aphrodisiac. Uneven first impressions don't mean anything, and affection gets evened out later. I am thankful every day I listened to Valerie and let her persuade me to take another look at Aaron. He and I seem to switch off between who is more devoted, yearly, monthly, and sometimes daily. Love is never a perfect science.

9

EXIT INTERVIEWS:
THE ULTIMATE FEEDBACK

Everyone always asks me why such a high percentage of my students get published during my classes every term. Mediabistro.com, one of the great places where I teach nonfiction writing, even joked in one of its ads that I paid off editors around the country to print all of my pupils' work to make me look good. (Ha! Like I could afford bribery on the teaching salary they pay me.) There is a secret to how it really works behind the scenes. On the first day I ask the class to write a three-page, double-spaced, first-person "humiliation essay" about the most humiliating thing that's ever happened to them. The second week, everyone hands in first drafts and a few brave souls offer to read their personal pieces out loud. When they are done, I offer my unadulterated opinion. That's what they are paying me for, so I don't hold back. I find my skills as a former book critic much more useful in a classroom. What good does it really do a writer to trash what's already in print, when it's too late to change anything? At this preliminary stage, the faultfinding serves a function.

I mark notes on their papers while I verbalize my honest, intense, critical assessment. It can be a painful process that once in a while leads to arguments, recriminations, sore feelings, and tears. I try to begin with something positive, such as "interesting idea," "perfect form," "I like your title," or "good energy." But fawning will not do anyone any good. In fact, it does people bad, encouraging illusions, impatience, and imperfection. It could lead to career sabotage, because if someone thinks his piece is terrific, he will send it out to an editor too early. Students can embarrass themselves, get rejected, get hurt, and ruin a connection with somebody important in one e-mail. So I'm a tough grader and commentator, focusing on what they are doing that does not work and how they can improve and fix it.

If somebody doesn't want to share work with the class, that person hands it to me and I edit the pages in pen, line by line. Although I'll put a star on a phrase or sentence that "sings," most of my feedback instructs them to prune, polish, purify, repair, reform, and reorganize more carefully. I cross out unneeded words that should be deleted, and put question marks by phrases I don't understand. In the margins I scrawl such standard editing comments as: "Needs better, timelier lead," "cut clichés and repetitions," "don't keep using the same words over and over," "add more topical references," "too obvious," "say something smarter, newer, fresher," "surprise me at the end."

This can be very difficult and disconcerting when the subject matter is extremely revealing. Many of the compositions chronicle divorces, breakups, family feuds, getting fired, dumped, or demeaned by someone they care about. I'm very analytic, so I'm not only dissecting their style, punctuation, and phrasing, but I'm also psychoanalyzing them at the same time, saying "that's too trite and easy," "don't question it, answer it," "stop avoiding the dicey issues you bring up," "don't be afraid to go there," "don't be a victim, challenge yourself more," and "dig deeper."

Students who hand in a rewrite a week later that completely ignores all of my recommendations are usually the ones who wind up having no luck with editors. They also alienate and bore me. I often write "don't waste my time" on top and give them their pieces back, unedited (since I already edited them once and they didn't trust me or listen). Conversely, my favorites every term are the eager beavers who carefully listen to the advice they are paying for, take my suggestions, and incorporate my corrections into their revisions. I'm not implying that I am always right. It's just that I've been doing this for twenty-five years and they've been doing it for twenty-five minutes. I've had hundreds of editors come speak to my classes about exactly what kind of work they will buy from somebody starting out. Plus it benefits me when students succeed. I feel smart and successful, I get a vicarious thrill, and most people who get published wind up taking my class again and recommending it to friends. Many former students land newspaper and magazine internships and jobs and then feel obligated to come back as a speaker for my current students.

If I had to make an overview chart that divided up which wannabes become worker bees with published clips and jobs, and which students remain frustrated, clip-less, and jobless, the outcome would come down to one difference: those who can take criticism versus those who can't take criticism. It works the same way with dating and mating.

Of course, when you ask someone's opinion on something new and personal that you're writing, wearing, or trying, you always want to hear "Bravo! Fantastic! Marvelous! More! You're going to be very successful very soon, I'm certain of it!" But if there is someone very encouraging you know who will always tell you, "Perfect! You're a genius! Don't change a thing!" go ask somebody else. A sycophant and two dollars will get you on the subway. There is only one way to really learn, grow, stretch, change, and transform yourself into a winner who gets what you want. You have to find, beg for, hear, listen, and take in the truth from an expert in the field who knows something that you don't yet know.

Sure, getting reviewed, roasted, repudiated, reproved, or rewritten is never fun. I ran out crying after my first NYU poetry workshop trashed a beloved early poem I'd delicately crafted. But I soon learned that "you have to kill your babies," which means getting rid of phrases you love so much that they stand out and overwhelm the rest of the work. The second draft of that poem was so much better, it soon found a home in a literary magazine. I not only got over my emotional fragility and developed a thicker skin, but I became dependent on that critical process. After I finished my master's degree, I so desperately craved the kind of literary judgment that went to the jugular that I started my own writing workshop, which lasted for eighteen years. Because I wanted to keep improving, I only extended invitations to critics and scholars I thought were smarter than me.

We made a rule that after reading work aloud, the author could not speak while we went around the room giving our critique. Talking back meant the author was too busy being defensive and thus not really listening. After everyone was done, I'd then say to the author, "Any comments?" Usually members would mumble, "Thanks. Needs work," or "Back to the drawing board." But after we commented on one fiction writer's story, I asked, "Any comments?" He said, "Yeah, you're all assholes." Everyone cracked up and applauded—because that's what it feels like to get ripped apart.

Yet despite how bad it initially feels, you have to force

yourself to find the right people to ask for feedback. Some-one sweet or soft-spoken, like your mother or your best friend, might not want to risk offending you. Or maybe she'll tell you what she really thinks—but in such a mild and sugarcoated way that it'll be easy to miss, dismiss, ig-nore, or distort. It's much smarter to find sharp critics in the universe who think highly enough of you to tell you the truth, the whole truth, and nothing but the truth. These straight-talking humans could save you years of mistakes, repeated idiocy, and confusion. Sometimes the harsher their words, the more profound, memorable, and helpful they will be to you in the long run.

I recall the time I decided that my subtle white business cards with black type were too boring. I wanted something that would stand out more, so I had cards made on black paper with metallic-looking silver lettering. I thought they were dazzling, but they were so different I wanted a second opinion. I showed them to my neighbor Olga, who thought they were cool. Then I realized that Olga thought every-thing I said and did was cool. So I showed my new calling cards to my more discerning architect friend Stacey, whom I'd grown up with. While I'd always been verbally astute, Stacey had a more sophisticated visual sensibility. She took one look at the unusual, flashy coloring on my recent pur-chase and said, "Oh, how cute. Stripper cards."

I looked at my brand-new black-and-silver creations and realized Stacey was sort of right. They were too garish, showy, and overdone for a freelance journalist and book critic who wanted to be taken seriously. So I'd wasted thirty dollars. Had I slipped one to a *New York Times Review of Books* editor, I could have lost face, assignments, and money. I might have even been the laughingstock of the highbrow journal. Refusing to throw out a thousand of them, I still sometimes give them out to my students and close friends.

Yet now as I pull them out of my briefcase, I say, "Here are my new stripper cards," owning up to my bad taste and appearing to be in on the joke. Thank God for Stacey and her tactless stance that she wasn't afraid to share with me. I've had several other instances where raw and disparaging reactions really improved my life.

While it's an accepted form of review in many fields—like writing, architecture, and medicine—most people don't realize that this kind of critical assessment also works wonders when it comes to romance. The reason I was able to get such a good groom, and now have such a close relationship with my husband, is that I asked for, and received, immense amounts of assistance from older and wiser love mentors who told me the naked truth. In times of chaos or confusion, their blunt lines echo through my mind, forming a funny poetic philosophy I live by. I still hear my matchmaker Valerie responding to my complaint that Aaron wasn't my type by saying, "Your type is neurotic, self-destructive, and not the least bit interested in you. Go out with him again." I often recall my therapist Dr. Gross instructing me: "Love doesn't make you happy. Make yourself happy" and "Everything you've always thought about love and marriage is wrong."

If you are a single man or woman who has not had satisfying results from your last twenty or thirty rendezvous, chances are it is not just the fault of all those others. It could be partly your fault too. But that doesn't mean you are a bad or unlovable person, or that you have an *X* written on your forehead. You aren't being punished for your past sins. Here's the rub: there might be something amiss in your process. It could be anything from the kind of partners you are pursuing, to how you are meeting, to your choice of clothes, impatience, laziness, lack of follow-up, or harboring expectations too high to live up to. You need to pull back, find out what's going wrong, and start figuring out how to make it go right. That's certainly a better plan than continuing to do whatever you are doing that isn't getting you what you want.

When you feel upset, addled, or at sea about why someone you liked never called you again, don't give up and decide it was just fate. Or that your date is a jerk or must want somebody who is younger, better-looking, hotter, more successful, or richer than you. That may very well be the case. But one of the beautiful aspects of having a matchmaker is that after the dinner, lunch, or drinks date is done, you are not alone. You have excellent options for communication and commiseration. So ask your fixer-upper to find out why the other party didn't think you would make a love match. As a matchmaker, I would never intentionally hurt somebody's feelings. Yet I would also never fake it in this situation. You don't ever want someone pining away for a person who was not the least bit interested.

If you are ready to face reality and gather fascinating facts about yourself, then contact your matchmaker to see if she can provide you with feedback. But even before you hear this new information, be prepared to feel attacked, aggravated, angry, annoyed, or hurt. You did not win this time. Perhaps you made mistakes you're not aware of. Someone was not charmed by you. Still, it's better to elucidate this enigma than be lied to. It will not do you any good to hear nice stuff about all of your great qualities. If your date thought you were that great, he would have phoned you again. He didn't. You need to figure out why.

If all you can handle is positive comments and encouragement, call your mother or kid sister, hang out with your old entourage, or hire a personal assistant or publicist to soothe your ego. You can always pay someone to blow smoke up your ass. But that will not make you a stronger, wiser, more charitable, or important person. Think of all the CEOs and celebrities who reveled in and believed their own hype and wound up alone, addicted, bankrupt, in jail, or dying young. Indeed, denying the truth and only listening to false praise could keep you solitary and stagnant.

Nor will it assist you to hear vague, cryptic excuses by those who rejected you. "I'm just not ready for much now" or "I'm not sure what I want" mean little and perhaps are used to sidestep the uncomfortable truth. Instead, ask for negative, hard-to-hear, fault-finding, disparaging, nitpicking, undisguised honesty—what your date really thought of your looks, body, clothes, social skills, personality, and performance. I hardly ever quote the Bible, but I do agree that "the truth shall set you free." If you can listen, nothing will teach you more and help you become a better, more conscious, humble, and aware human being. You can't fix your social status until you find out how others see you, and learn where you can improve.

How to Send Your Fixer-Upper on a Fact-Finding Mission

- First make sure you've expressed gratitude toward your matchmaker for the initial introduction and try to get information this way. "Thanks again for that fun blind date. I haven't heard from Ken, but it really was so sweet of you to think of me," might prompt her to say, "Oh yeah, he went to Europe on a business trip. But I'll find out what he thinks when he gets back next week."

- Sometimes you have to ask nicely, and very clearly, for feedback. If "what do you think he thought of me?" doesn't elicit any action, be more specific. "I was wondering if you would do me a huge favor and ask Ken why he didn't call me again."

- Now follow up with your fix-up fanatic. If you don't hear back the first time, it's okay to try again by phone or e-mail. The squeaky wheel does get the grease. Though make sure you sound sweet and squeaky, and not desperate and bitter.

- Flattery and flowers never hurt. You could be asking your matchmaker to do something unusual or uncomfortable for her. Perhaps she feels she went out of her way for you already. If you get this vibe, write a thank-you card, reminding her how much you appreciated her help. Little gestures like sending flowers, candy, or a candle can mean a lot. I always remember my student who left a six-pack of Diet Coke Caffeine Free with a ribbon around it with my doorman. (It only cost her a few dollars to make a memorable impression and make me want to help her more.)

- Say good things about the date. Even though they eventually split up, my former student Tammy thanked me profusely for introducing her to Aaron's friend Adam. She said that he had a lot of integrity and that she'd had a lot of fun with him in the three months they'd dated. This is an especially nice thing to do when the blind date was your fixer-upper's relative, boss, colleague, or close friend. Tammy's gracious attitude impressed me so much that when she left, I e-mailed Ralph, a handsome, single artist friend of mine, and told him basically, "Have I got a girl for you . . ."

- Let your matchmaker know your motives. You might get better results if you relate that you're looking for honest feedback to improve yourself and your luck. Most people are impressed by someone who is really trying. Who knows? Perhaps your fixer-upper will throw in what she really thinks of your latest haircut or outfit too. Yes, everyone's taste is different, but your matchmaker is invested in helping you find a partner and you haven't had any luck on your own. So at least listen and consider the criticism.

- Make it clear that you're not a stalker. Promise that you will not repeat any of the information that your matchmaker relays to you. And reassure your fixer-upper that you will not contact your ex-date again inappropriately.

- Make sure to keep your promise. One downside of going through matchmakers is that they usually hear about your romantic antics—from the person they fixed you up with.

Criticism Can Elicit Hurt and Anger

After a dinner I thought went well with a handsome corporate lawyer, he never called me again. Since he was so terrific looking, I assumed he was not attracted to me and, because of my own insecurities at the time, decided it was because I wasn't thin enough. Two weeks after that dinner date, I asked Rina, the mutual friend who'd introduced us, to find out why he had never called me again. Rina called me a few days later to share what he'd said. It seemed that Lawyerman had indeed found me physically attractive and sexy. But he complained that all I talked about all night was my work. He said it gave him a headache and he couldn't wait to get away from me. Ouch! So the problem wasn't my body, but my big mouth.

Hearing this first felt like a stab in my heart. What did he mean, I talked about my work too much? Rina must have been wrong, I thought defensively. But then I replayed the date in my brain. I did tell him the details of a fantastic interview I just did for the *New York Times Magazine*. I thought it would impress him. It impressed me. How could anyone not be interested in my upcoming article for the *New York Times Magazine*? But I held my tongue and didn't trash him, or call him up to say he was a sexist, boring lawyer clown who couldn't handle a real woman with a brain, as I felt like doing.

I knew from experience that it was smarter to be able to stay with, hear, and contemplate criticism. Ultimately, I was glad to know what my date thought of me because my vanity about my appearance was stronger than my vanity about my personality. Rather than assuming that he was too superficial and needed someone who looked like a model, it was much more helpful to know that I had blown the date—not with my looks, but with my personality. It's too boring to play victim. Plus it rarely gets you anywhere but more victimized. And you know what? I later realized that the lawyer who never became my lover was absolutely right! I did talk about my work the whole night. It was a bad habit that I still haven't quite gotten over. This led me to figure out some new facts about myself and the way I conducted social interactions.

Here are some questions to ponder about the way you might be conducting yourself without realizing it.

- Are you talking about yourself, your work, or your hobbies nonstop during the first meeting, when you are with someone who doesn't know you and might not share your interests?

- In order to impress a new person, are you coming across as a show-off or braggart?

- Are you revealing too much information too soon about your dubious past, former relationships, or therapy, making your date uncomfortable?

- Are you reciting your résumé? Why? Are you expecting praise for your accomplishments from someone you hardly know?

- It's great to be funny, opinionated, and spicy. But are you trashing your ex-lovers, family members, colleagues, or friends in a way that isn't appropriate or might scare or alienate someone you just met?

- Are you afraid of silence or any lull in the conversation and rushing to fill it in?

- Are you asking enough questions about your date's life, career, and interests?

- Although it's great to love who you are, or what you do, is there a way to come across as more self-deprecating, modest, or humble?

- Are you stating your political or cultural opinions so strongly that there isn't room for another point of view?

- Would you do better socially by hanging out with people in the same field as you? Or those in a completely different arena?

- Do you blame your imperfect looks or body for your failures when perhaps your problems are due to something you have much more control over, such as a pushy and overbearing personality?

If your matchmaker does not want to follow up for you, or tries but has no luck gathering any specific interesting feedback, is it ever appropriate for you to ask a former suitor yourself what went wrong? Here's a hint: Yes! It can be very illuminating to ask people you dated once—or many times—what they thought of you.

In the middle of a serious midlife crisis, five years after I married Aaron, I even called and met with the five long-term ex-boyfriends who had hurt me the most. I asked them what really had gone wrong when we split up. It was a cathartic experience that solved all kinds of mysteries that had confused me for years. The quest led to my memoir *Five Men Who Broke My Heart*, and then to an amazing fan letter.

After finishing my book about reconnecting with lost loves, a fifty-five-year-old Manhattan banker named Michelle Mead decided to contact John Armor, the North Carolina lawyer to whom she'd been engaged when she was a senior at Goucher College in Baltimore thirty-three years earlier. When they remet, Michelle found out he was still dashing, recently separated, and greatly regretted his past mistakes. He wound up proposing. Her missive ended "John is especially pleased that, having my broken my heart, he got a chance to repair it."

So along with blind dates, consider finding out if your favorite old lovers are currently single, what their perspective was, and if it might have changed with time.

The Right Way to Encourage Ex-Repartee

If you decide to contact someone you dated in the past, be sure that you approach this person appropriately, with class and grace, and for good reasons.

- Showing up at your ex-date's doorstep, gym, or favorite hangout is never, ever a smart move. It could lead to a bad scene if his new date, spouse, child, or parent is with him. Even if he is alone, you could literally get a door slammed in your face. He could assume you want sex and lunge at you. He could not recognize you and hurt your feelings. He could grab a weapon, thinking you are a burglar. He could call the police and have you arrested for trespassing. In other words: don't even think about it.

- Be as subtle and unobtrusive as possible. Whether it's three weeks, three years, or three decades later, a polite letter or card, or a kind e-mail, is the best way to initiate contact. It would be self-defeating to try before three weeks is up because it doesn't give your date a chance to call you again. Don't launch into the exit interview during the first few sentences. Ask if this is an okay time first.

- Be short and sweet. I know blog culture thinks spilling thousands of words daily proves your literary prowess. But now is not the time to write a novel-length treatise on your ideas of love and romance in modern America. Nor is it a good idea to confess your intense passionate crush or heartbreak, or share your last seventeen therapy sessions. This is a person who did not choose to sit across the table from you and have another drink. He does not want to hear about your feelings. He is doing you a big favor by answering your e-mail. Brevity is the soul of wit and self-preservation. "How's it going? I was wondering if you'd have a few minutes to speak on the phone" is about the right word length.

- If he says he was planning to get in touch with you again, he was just busy, don't believe him. If he was going to contact you, he probably would have contacted you by now. On the other hand, do not say, "You're full of shit. If you were going to call me by now, you already would have." Keep your expectations very low.

- Do not be combative or accuse your former date of any wrongdoing whatsoever. Even if she said, "I'll call you" and didn't, she was just trying to be polite. It is each person's prerogative to decide who she wants to date again. If anything, act grateful that she is willing to help you out with this project. Don't be a victim, be a researcher of human behavior trying to solve a mystery you don't yet understand.

- Do research first. By asking your matchmaker what she's heard or by looking up someone on Google, you might find data that elucidates everything. This could include learning about his new love, spouse, children, divorce, a recent move or job promotion, a new project, or a recent interview published about him. Once in a while you might uncover something essential that did not occur to you. For example, instead of rejecting you, what if he wound up in the hospital with a sudden illness? Or one of his parents or relatives died and he flew to Atlanta for the funeral? If this is the case, sending a card expressing concern is always kind and appropriate. (Though don't expect an answer.)

- Whenever possible, be funny and self-deprecating.

- Be unusually accommodating. If someone agrees to speak with you, be willing to do it on his time and your dime. When I contacted my five exes for my book research, one only wanted to answer questions by e-mail. That turned out to be a fabulous way to discuss what happened between us.

- If your ex-date doesn't respond to you after your first attempt, hang it up. Do not try again. Becoming a stalker or a masochist will not be an enriching or an encouraging experience. It will make you feel worse about yourself, which will make meeting someone new even harder.

- Trying to get back together—or convince someone he should date you again—is never the right reason to phone an ex-date or ex-lover. If this is your motivation, adopt a puppy or call a shrink or close friend who will talk you out of it.

- Don't make any contact when you are depressed, angry, bitter, or upset. If you are feeling embarrassed, humiliated, rejected, or dejected, spending time with your family, closest friends, pets, or therapist will make you feel better. Contacting a date who didn't phone you again—even if you are polite and discreet—will only make you feel more embarrassed, humiliated, rejected, or dejected.

- If you ask questions, listen to the answers. If someone agrees to talk with you on the phone, in person, or by e-mail, do not be defensive and dismiss, interrupt, or argue. In fact, keep your mouth shut and your opinions to yourself. Give yourself time to hear and process what she is saying.

- Discuss and analyze the result later with a trusted party. This can be your matchmaker, your best friend, your mother, or your sibling. Again, do not defensively start trashing what has been said about you, or begging the trusted party to tell you it isn't true. If you yell, "I don't babble incoherently about my work all the time, do I?" you are putting your point person on the spot to lie and respond, "Of course you don't." If instead you calmly ask, "Do you ever think I talk about my work too much?" someone might come clean and say something helpful like, "Sometimes I do

think that too. It makes me feel like you're not interested in my job or my life."

- Turn negatives into positives. If two people tell you
that you don't listen well, this could be an important
criticism to acknowledge about yourself. It can easily
lead you to apply a new, better way of interacting that
involves asking others more questions about themselves. If you come across as interested, people will
find you much more interesting. Knowing this could
wind up illuminating other mysteries in your life.
Could it be why you've had trouble landing or keeping friends and jobs? Maybe it'll help you get a raise or
a higher position or make a better impression on the
next potential landlord, boss, or friend you approach.

- Stay with the pain. The process of asking exes what
they really think of you and your past relationship can
be uncomfortable, awkward, confusing, agonizing, humiliating, and insulting. It can take a while before
their words really sink in and you can comprehend
what it all means. Ultimately it will be a helpful way to
understand your past and unblock you for the future.

- Now go away and focus on someone or something
else. This interview is a one-shot deal. If the person
from your past miraculously later decides to check up
on you, or ask you out again, or wants to be friends,
maybe more contact might come out of it. But if he
doesn't contact you again, do not contact him, but
move on. If you must keep analyzing it, hash it out
with your best friend, mother, or matchmaker.

- Figure out how the experience can work to your benefit.
This way the entire interaction will be worthwhile and
you can make sure that you don't make the same mis-

takes again. If all else fails, pull out your journal and take notes. Remember many a great song, play, dance, novel, memoir, poem, essay, short story, movie, move, and major life change was motivated by a little heartache.

Fair Questions to Ask Your Ex-Date

Yes, people of the opposite sex can be silly, dumb, or out of touch. Problem is, you want one. And the last one you picked isn't picking you. Even if your date's limitations or issues are to blame, you're the one with the bad pattern you want to break. So your preferences are suspect. I found that even that lawyer I had one date with—someone I didn't care much about at all—was able to teach me something about myself. By asking your former dates the following questions, you aren't giving them too much power. By listening carefully to their answers, you might give yourself the power to change.

- What were you told about me before meeting?
- Did you find it to be a fair description?
- Was there a particular reason you decided to give our blind date a shot?
- Did I seem friendly and nice when we connected by e-mail or telephone?
- Did you feel I was dressed and acted appropriately on our date?
- Did my smoking, drinking, or eating habits seem appropriate?
- Did you find we didn't have any chemistry?
- Was there anything I did that you found the least bit insensitive or annoying?
- What did you like best about me?

- Were there ways I seemed to be trying too hard or not hard enough?
- Was there any particular reason you decided not to contact me again?
- Is there anything you can suggest that I could change about myself to make someone feel more comfortable on first meeting?
- Did you feel obligated to say, "I'll call you," when you didn't really mean it?
- Does it make you uncomfortable that I'm contacting you now?

Hard Things You Might Hear

- I did not feel physically attracted to you.
- I expected someone taller/thinner/younger/older/more professional.
- I tend to go out with thinner, more athletic types.
- You seem too old/young/conservative/liberal/sexually aggressive or not sexually aggressive enough for me.
- My ex-lover called me and I realized it's not really over.
- I don't go out with smokers/drinkers/gamblers/meat eaters.
- You came late and I'm always on time.
- You took two calls from your cell phone, which I found rude.
- You didn't ask me any questions about myself.
- I could tell you were not attracted to me.
- I didn't realize you'd been divorced two times/had three kids/lived in another country/weren't yet divorced, which was a turnoff.

- You mentioned you don't want children and I do.

- You trashed your ex in an angry way that was alienating.

- You didn't offer to treat or share the bill, which both-ered me.

- You didn't put me in a cab/offer to walk me home/invite me in, which I took to mean you weren't interested.

Again, if someone is kind enough to take the time to an-swer these questions, do not interrupt, argue, discuss, or dismiss anything said out of hand. Indeed during this phone call, you should merely listen very closely, take notes, and try to be objective and gracious. Afterward, do not respond to any allegations or try to keep the conversation going any longer. Few people come off well when they feel surprised, ambushed, criticized, or hurt. Instead thank the person profusely and wish him or her well.

Then spend some time thinking about what was said be-fore you respond further. Before taking action, discuss it with your matchmaker, best friend, sibling, or therapist. There may be a miscommunication or misunderstanding worth clearing up. If your date thought you weren't interested, and you really were, clarifying in a sweet card or e-mail might be appropriate. If you realize you did something rude—like show up late, take two cell phone calls during the meal, or try to shove your tongue down her throat at the end—by all means apologize. If there is a good reason, you can briefly explain your transgression. Even if you already said it at the time of the date, it won't hurt to once again say, "I'm so sorry the traffic made me an hour late," or, "I'm sorry I had to pick up my cell phone when it was my babysitter or boss calling." But it is not appropriate to be surly, blustery, or argumenta-tive, or try to justify bad behavior.

If you had too many drinks and came on too frisky, but

hope for another shot, try an atonement/flattery combo, such as "I'm sorry, you're just so gorgeous, I didn't mean to get carried away." Then be perfectly prudish on the next *two dates* to prove you are not an animal. It's also fine to use humor to sweetly try to cajole away someone's minor criticism or hesitations, but tread lightly. When my friend Serena told Roger it made her nervous that he'd been married twice, he kept telling her, "You can't call me a commitment-phobe" and "Well, at least I'm not afraid to walk down the aisle." He supplemented his argument for himself with calls, sincere conversations, invitations for dates, flowers, and gifts. She eventually bought his explanations and he ended up walking down the aisle a third time—with her.

Whatever you do, don't lie—to your date or to yourself. Sometimes your actions tell the truth more than your words do. If someone is sure he wants children and already senses that you don't, don't hold back your true feelings. If your date is a nonsmoker who can't be with a smoker and you smoke, don't pretend you've quit if you haven't. I once did this and it led to a comedy of errors on a second date where I faked food poisoning in order to keep running out to sneak cigarettes, spraying perfume, and eating breath mints the whole night. Ultimately it just wasn't worth it to fake it.

If the person just told you that he wasn't attracted to you, didn't feel chemistry, realized he still loved his ex, or only wanted a twenty-five-year-old Catholic vegetarian (and you're a forty-year-old Protestant meat eater), accept it. Do not try to talk him into liking you or end with, "I'll call you," "I hope to see you again," or "Call me if you change your mind." He probably won't.

However, you can change your own mind. Sometimes the only remedy is action. Instead of crying, being pissed off, or giving up, take the new information that your matchmaker or blind date just replayed and consider doing it differently next time. Even transforming something small or trivial on your next date could empower you and restack the odds in your favor. Here are some suggestions to mull over.

- As an experiment, don't talk as much during your next lunch or dinner and instead listen and ask more questions.

- Instead of having drinks or dinner, which puts you on the spot and makes you nervous, next time consider a fun activity you enjoy, like bowling, tennis, or miniature golf.

- If the fancy restaurant or formal party your date chose made you uncomfortable, next time speak up earlier and suggest someplace more casual and comfortable for you, perhaps in your neighborhood.

- If big parties make you feel invisible, only meet dates one-on-one from now on, especially when you feel your brains and sense of humor come across better this way.

- If you haven't felt physically attracted to any of the suitors your matchmaker set you up with, next time try to meet singles at parties, readings, or benefits so you don't feel as stuck.

- Stop chasing great-looking younger people who care too much about age, looks, and body. Try someone your own age or older.

- If you are only attracted to great-looking, buff younger people, decide to lose weight and start exercising more to improve your looks and body so you can compete in that realm.

- Make an appointment with a new hairstylist, a makeup artist, or a stylist who can revamp your wardrobe.

- Decide to open up your search to people of different backgrounds. If you are a thirty-year-old Jewish lawyer, and haven't had luck dating Jewish lawyers in their thirties, tell your matchmaker you will now go on dates with anyone nice.

- If you decide people you've been meeting in your area are too superficial for you, volunteer, join a religious group, take an Outward Bound trip, or become a Peace Corps worker in order to meet deeper, more socially conscious people.

- Even if you feel your date had no right to comment on your personal habits, limit your drinking, smoking, or overeating on your next date to see if it feels any different.

- If you can't stop drinking, smoking, or overeating on your own, go to a session with a therapist or addiction specialist, or attend a meeting of AA, SmokEnders, or Weight Watchers—just to see what you think.

- Wear a different kind of outfit on your next date. If you usually don all black, try a color. If you usually wear plaid pants, try a suit. If you're usually conservative, be bolder. If you don't know how, ask a friend or family member to help you out.

- If many dates in a row have been a disaster, perhaps it's time to take some time off from dating and just hang out with friends and family. Or plan a vacation to rest and reenergize yourself.

- Put yourself on the line more than usual. If you haven't heard from your date after a week, e-mail a casual "Thanks for the drink. It was really nice to meet you," even if you're a woman who usually doesn't call men after a first date. If you phoned your blind date right after the fix-up and she never returned your call, try one more time. Send her a Christmas, New Year's, Valentine's Day, Easter, or Passover card, just saying "Hi. Happy holiday. Hope all is well."

- Extend invitations. The perk of planning big charity benefits, hosting events and readings, and throwing parties is that you can invite hundreds of people to come and not have to spend hours entertaining each one. So if you ever have a date with someone decent—even if he never called back, or called back too soon or too often, or told your matchmaker he wasn't attracted to you—you could pursue him platonically. Who knows? Don't be shortsighted. He might donate to your charity, give you a job, sell you a great apartment, or become the mate of one of your friends—which would all wind up benefiting you in the long run.

10

HOW TO STAY SINGLE FOREVER

Several sophisticated and sexy single girlfriends of mine tell me they are dying to find partners. Yet here are their strategies for meeting and treating mankind:

Typecast: They have many specific requirements for age, height, weight, salary, profession, hair color, race, and religion and don't ever deviate—even when it always ends up a dead end. My friend Lori likes artsy men and wants a ponytailed guitar player in tight jeans and leather jacket who lives in her neighborhood. When I suggest that Lori be more open-minded, she says I'm right. Maybe she'll try a ponytailed musician in tight jeans and leather jacket who lives six miles away.

Fear Even Cyberintimacy: Carol, a forty-four-year-old redheaded copywriter, says, "Only losers go on fix-ups." So she says no to her pals, family members, and coworkers who want to set her up on blind dates with real men they've met. Instead she meets guys through the Internet, pretending that cruising the Web isn't the blindest dating yet. She posts a picture where she's eight years younger and twenty pounds thinner, lies about her age, postponing any actual meeting in favor of being pen pals, writing long letters where she describes herself as "an honest, real person who's been hurt by previous deceptions," and says she's "looking for someone equally sincere and down-to-earth."

Share Everything: My colleague Claire, a forty-one-year-old voluptuous, dark-haired writer, believes in complete honesty. So she tells Tony about her abortions, therapy, past anorexia and bulimia, deep-rooted insecurities, drug and alcohol problems, and her dysfunctional family. She also goes on and on about such gynecological issues as her cramps, previous STDs, and latest yeast infection on their second date.

Have Sex within a Week: Claire jumped into Tony's bed before she figured out whether her new partner was married, wanted by the law, healthy, or had the same sexual preference that she did. She assumed three orgasms meant it was love at last and freaked out when he didn't phone within twenty-four hours.

Care What Others Think: Lori finally did meet a cute musician named Jake. But her roommate and friends didn't think he was all that sexy. So she decided she wasn't into him. No matter that Jake was honest and sweet. Other people's criticisms of your dates should always be taken into account. Don't bother to examine their motives or notice if they are miserably single and prefer you to stay miserable too.

Overemphasize Looks: Jill, an actress, despises men who care about a woman's breast size, but then refuses to be seen with a man who is three inches shorter than she, balding, bearded, twelve years older than she is, or eight pounds overweight.

Compare: Now that Tony called Claire, she's not so sure she wants him. She constantly harps on the fact that Tony isn't as brilliant as her ex, Phillip, whom she left when he got another woman pregnant. She keeps saying that she misses Phillip's huge penis, forgetting that he stuck it in another woman while they were still dating.

Assume He Reads Minds: When Jill met Paul, she didn't think it was necessary to tell him she was fanatical about condoms because Harry, her last fling, left her with herpes. Last week she forgot to tell Paul that the reason she was in a bad mood was that she'd blown her last big audition. When Paul asked, "What's wrong?" she said, "Nothing." She figures that if he really cared, he'd understand.

Try to Change Everything about Your Amour as Soon as Possible: When Lori decided to give sweet guitar-playing Jake a second chance, she insisted that he join a gym, get into therapy, get a new haircut, and wear the new clothes she bought him. Of course, at the same time, she says she needs a man who'll love her for who she really is.

Sleep with Old Lovers: If your new partner is too slow, triangles are always good for drama. Jill had a few racy rendezvous with her former guy, Harry, the one who couldn't commit to a one-night stand, and still owes her money he promised he'd pay for the medication to treat the STD he'd left her with.

Obsess about Your Physical Flaws: Lori turns off the lights in the bedroom every time she has sex because she's gained six pounds. Claire wears four-inch heels everywhere since she's self-conscious she's only five feet two. They don't give a thought to the millions of women in the world who are short, overweight, plain-looking, happily married, and quiet about their imperfections.

Share Your Timetable: In the third week of keeping company, in the name of honesty, Claire tells Tony that she wants to have a child, preferably with someone she is married to, by this time next year.

Don't Change: Jill says it's easy to be attracted to unfaithful men and the last three just happened to be recovering alcoholics like her father. Lori thinks soul-searching is too much of a downer. Carol and Claire agree that therapy rarely works and it's too expensive anyway. So when they find themselves single again, they say all men are dogs and blame it on fate.

Biggest Love Blockades

Superficialitis: This illness makes you so caught up in finding someone with certain looks, money, or social status that you only wind up with perfect-looking rich Ivy League losers and thus cheat yourself out of true love. Analyze why you need somebody so gorgeous, so rich, or so Harvard beside you. Could it be because you are insecure about your own looks, status, career, earning power, or worthiness?

Stinginess: If you just desperately need to wed youthful eye candy, then get real, open your wallet, and swallow the trade-off. Big-shot male CEOs keep their gorgeous young trophy wives in luxury. They also pay through the teeth for previous divorces, alimony for their other exes, and therapy for their deserted children. After my friend Geoff moved in with his new, skinny, and beautiful girlfriend, he asked her to pay half the rent. She moved out. Geoff, a Woody Allen type, was confused. "If you want an equal partner who'll pay her share, stop chasing *Playboy* bunnies," I told him. "If you want a *Playboy* bunny, then play the sugar daddy." According to the *New York Post*, when Melania Trump was asked if she'd marry The Donald if he weren't rich, she answered, "Would he marry me if I wasn't young and beautiful?"

It works for both sexes. Many female glamour-pusses provide more of the money and fame than their handsome younger studs, who are less rich and famous. But be aware that you often get what you pay for.

Being Starstruck (or the Maureen Dowd Syndrome): Just because you can date or sleep with someone famous or powerful doesn't mean you can marry someone famous or powerful. Even if you've had fascinating relationships with luminaries, ask yourself if during those fascinating relationships, they were also in various stages of separation, divorce, engagement, marriage, and procreation with other partners. If so, then get over it and have dinner with a nice Connecticut dentist. If you forget to work through your psychological issues, you could wake up at fifty-three years old bemoaning the national crises of men not willing to wed successful women. In reality there are many brilliant women with graduate degrees, awards, nice husbands, and children. They just had the good sense to get the stars out of their eyes and go for a real guy they could wed in their twenties, thirties, or forties.

Perfectionism: This kind of successful, romantic idealist has no room for mistakes or imperfections. So when the person she is dating forgets to make a big fuss for her birthday, Christmas, and Valentine's Day, it's over. Somebody who has all kinds of rules about how everything must be won't allow herself—or her mate—to be human. The only perfect love in the world is onscreen or in the pages of romantic poetry. Meanwhile, look up how messy and insane the poets' and actors' relationships were in real life.

Truly Blind Dating: It's nice to think highly of yourself. But sometimes what seems like high self-esteem is actually self-distortion. The simple truth is that people go for partners who look, act, and live like they do. I had an obese girlfriend who begged me to fix her up. Since she was charming and smart, I figured no problem. I invited her to parties and book events. But she only went for skinny, handsome men and would not even consider a man her size. Twice she pursued extremely buff boys, then was heartbroken when they were only interested in a platonic relationship with her. Yes, some people who aren't that young, thin, or good looking have found gorgeous, slender, or youthful mates. Mostly not. I would never tell anybody she had to lose weight or get a makeover or new job in order to find a spouse. But if you want a beauty, be a beauty. Or take a risk and reread the entry at the start of this section on stinginess.

Being Too Scared or Scarred: If your last relationship ended with your partner dying, divorcing, deserting or abusing you, it often takes a lot of time to mend and be ready to get out there again. If on your first fix-up you find yourself crying, spewing forth venom about your ex, or finding fault with everything your blind date says or does, you have an "I'm Too Wounded" sign on your forehead. Go home and call a good friend or a good shrink. Once you heal a bit more, you'll be much better company.

Self-Deception: A guy friend of mine dated and rejected many women over a decade, claiming they weren't pretty or thin enough. Then, in therapy, he realized he was in denial about being gay. Sexual confusion isn't so uncommon, but it can be dangerous and unfair to others. Men on the "down low" can spread AIDS and other diseases to their un-suspecting mates. A woman I know switched back and forth between male and female partners, alienating both sexes and hurting a child in the process. I have fixed up people who are straight, gay, and bisexual, and I believe everyone is entitled to love, marriage, and procreation. But singles should be honest with potential partners and themselves. You can be ambivalent and make a decision. So just pick a gender and stick with it. If you're too confused, be fair to the rest of us and remain celibate until you're sure. Or find someone like-minded and be clear and open about your preferences.

Self-Hatred: Self-esteem is never an external gift you can get from someone or something else. You must work hard to be happy within yourself. It's cliché, but you really must love yourself before you will be able to let somebody else love you. Waking up in the morning and hating what you see in the mirror is not an original feeling or horrific aber-ration. We're human; it happens all the time. But instead of inflicting it on someone else, face your issues and imperfec-tions first. The moment you fix yourself, and feel absolutely fine living alone with no mate, is often the exact moment you'll attract the right one.

11

THE TWELVE COMMANDMENTS
OF BLIND DATING

1. Do Not Flake Out, Cancel Last Minute, Keep Re-
   scheduling, Show Up Late, or Flee: Switching your
   dinner plans six times, or showing up at the restaurant
   where you agreed to meet forty-five minutes after the
   time you decided on, will not make you look popular,
   busy, or charming. Neither will faking a cell phone
   emergency so you can excuse yourself after five minutes. These rude actions will make you come off selfish
   and uncaring and will hurt the other person's feelings.
   Making someone sit alone for an hour at a dim-lit place
   waiting for you is semi-sadistic, especially if you grab a
   look at him and exit stage left. Even if you feel confused, uncomfortable, or ambivalent, you can still go
   through with the evening. In fact, it's an excellent exercise to commit to being your best self for one hour, regardless of whether you click romantically with this
   new person. Be respectful and patient. Think of a blind
   date as a multipurpose interview. If you don't get a

spouse out of the deal, you could get a job, work contact, apartment, lawyer, business partner, party invitation, or friendship. One wannabe actress I set up with a theater producer came away from their first date with the promise of an audition. And remember, I wound up passing on three of the nice men I dated to girlfriends whom they later married. So you could even be meeting your matchmaker without knowing it.

2. Do Not Show Up Badly Groomed: Unless your already-agreed-upon game plan is to take a Pilates class together at the gym, sweatpants and sweatshirts are not appropriate attire for a first connection. Unless you are both eighteen-year-old artists, ripped clothes are not such a great idea. Unless you look like Brad Pitt or Kate Moss, being unshaven with unwashed hair, dirty clothes, bad breath, or no makeup is not recommended either. On the other hand, too much perfume, cologne, makeup, fancy clothes, or jewelry could make you look like you're trying too hard. Present yourself the way you would for the owner of a house you want to rent or buy, the head of admissions at a prestigious school you want your child to attend, or a boss whose company you want to work for.

3. Do Not Lie: If you are embarrassed about your age, job, weight, finances, past relationships, or living situation, it's okay to be evasive on the first meeting. If your date asks direct questions you don't want to answer, make a joke and say, "A southerner never reveals such secrets," or ask, "Why do you want to know that?" or say, "Boy, you New Yorkers get personal right away, don't you?" These coy evasions are better than blatant deceptions, which could come back to haunt you. Upon hearing the age of Mr. X, one of the women I fixed up got nervous

that she was three years his senior. So she lied and said she was his age too. She kept the lie going as they dated for three years. Right before their wedding weekend, she worked herself into a frenzy, sure that he would call it all off when he learned the truth. He didn't call it off, saying it didn't matter. But it was hard for him to completely trust her afterward, and weddings are stressful enough without last-minute confessions.

4. **Do Not Divide Your Attention:** I'll never forget the trader I dated who kept taking phone calls on his cell, telling me, "Sorry, it's business." So this guy had to count his money four times over dinner? I never dated him again and am not surprised to hear that he's still single. Unless you are an ob-gyn on call for the mother of triplets, or have young children you're worried about or a close relative in the hospital, you can live for an hour without taking phone calls, pages, or checking your e-mail. Turn off your phone and your pager and put away your BlackBerry, laptop, and all other machinery. Even if the person across the table from you is not your eternal lover, she is also giving you her time and energy. If you keep acting as if your life is more important, you might wind up spending the rest of it alone.

5. **Do Not Trash Yourself:** I know honesty and a self-deprecating sense of humor can be terrific traits. Yet too many people too quickly share the inside scoop about their fat thighs, big noses, bad surgeries, and dental disasters on a first date. Furthermore, a brand-new person does not need to know about your history with antidepressants, psychostrippers, legal issues, drug or alcohol addictions, abortions, multiple exes, or family illnesses. Spilling inappropriate details about

your traumas way too soon is a way to subconsciously sabotage any chance of romance. I'll never forget when I invited my friend Sheila to dine with a group of friends, seating her next to Ted, an eligible bachelor. Sheila blurted out, "Boy, do I need a drink tonight. My dad's in the hospital with a broken back and my Prozac prescription just ran out." Ted ran out of the restaurant—literally—to get a cab home the first second he got. (Not surprisingly, Ted is now married to a very discreet woman, and Sheila is still single.) We all have problems and I applaud the need to come clean about dark episodes from your past, especially when it involves addiction, divorces, and depression. I'm not suggesting you lie. Just try to save your most bizarre, twisted secrets for your therapist, AA group, family, best friends, and journal. If you feel you must divulge these facts to the person you were just fixed up with, wait until the third, fourth, or fifth date. Or else you might never get a third, fourth, or fifth date.

6. Do Not Trash Your Exes: Last year I fixed up Lance, a very successful colleague, with a former student of mine named Betty. They were both going through difficult divorces. Afterward, Lance reported to me that he found Betty pretty, sexy, smart, and funny. But she said so many truly horrible things about her former husband, the father of her two children, that it scared Lance off completely. Yes, her former partner is a creep and they are in the middle of a terrible court battle. But the acrimonious divorce would have been easier for Betty to handle if she had a nice new companion behind the scenes to hold her hand. Now she doesn't. The way a new person talks about her ex might be the way she will

talk about you one day. If you hold your tongue and venom on your first date, something sweeter might wind up taking its place.

I recently set Lance up with my neighbor Lisa, who is also going through a divorce. Lisa's ex-husband is no less creepy than Betty's former spouse. But Lisa has a rule never to trash the daddy of her kids in public. Want to place bets on whether Betty or Lisa will be the first to remarry?

7. **Do Not Trash Your Matchmaker:** Evan was an attractive editor whom my friend Sandra hooked me up with. Sandra said she'd initially had a crush on him herself, but he wasn't really interested. So they became chums and she soon met her husband elsewhere. When I casually asked Evan, "So how do you and Sandra know each other?" he replied, "We used to be fuck buddies." Those were his exact words. I wanted to throw up. I couldn't believe that a supposedly intelligent man would say that to anybody, let alone Sandra's good friend. I didn't care that they used to sleep together. Sandra hadn't lied about it, she had merely omitted a few nights from her past that might have embarrassed her. I certainly had a few former flings I didn't advertise. I had nothing against people who sexually "hook up," become "friends with privileges," or recycle romance. But it was my woman pal's prerogative whether or not to divulge those details to me. A gentleman never tells. Had Evan subtly said, "We used to date but then became friends," I wouldn't have thought twice. But after crudely calling my friend "his fuck buddy," I never went out with him again. To this day when I see him, I remember.

8. **Do Not Make Split-Second Decisions Based on Super-ficial Data:** Okay, so your date disappoints you immedi-

ately because he or she is not tall, skinny, gorgeous, perfect, young, rich, brilliant, well dressed, well endowed, hairy, hairless, or hip enough. Just remember that all single people have fantasies about the ideal winner they will wind up with. Then there are the realistic souls who find human mates to procreate and live happily ever after with. Put negative thoughts out of your brain and find things you like about your blind date. Take a risk. Along with sitting there for at least a full hour, give this person a chance to win you over. Ask questions, be interesting and interested, open-minded, generous, and gracious. The skill of charming new people will only benefit you in the long run.

9. Do Not Ignore Dangerous Data: If the phrases *heroin addict, my jail stint, before my third divorce, after my second suicide attempt, my orgy phase, my problem with abusive behavior, my estranged children, rampant alcoholism, my untreated schizophrenia, my sexually transmitted disease, my inability to be intimate,* or *my eternal bisexuality* turn you off, good. They should turn you off! Still, unless you feel like you are in danger, don't be rude and run away. But don't make another plan, or give out your work or home address. Calmly contact your matchmaker to find out more facts on the matter. Maybe your fixer-upper didn't know all the details. Or maybe she had good reason to believe that all your date's problems were in the past. (This is why I suggest using e-mail and cell phones upon first contact and meeting only in a public place.)

10. Do Not Assume Hard Work and Love Are Incompatible: Donald Trump recently told a reporter that if you need couples therapy or Viagra, you married the wrong person. This is coming from a man who divorced two

wives with four children, and just had child number five in marriage number three to a girl roughly the age of his daughter. In other words: *consider the source.* Many singles similarly assume that when the right person comes along, there will be instant chemistry and it will all be easy sailing. Not so!!! Having to work to make conversation, fight your instincts to flee, stop being overly critical, or feel comfortable together is completely natural—especially as you get older and more set in your ways. Sometimes it can take a while. Aaron's close friends Jeff and Sue, one of the happiest married matches we know, said they had to meet three different times before it took. I dated Aaron for three months, then we broke up for three years, then we dated for three more years before we walked down the aisle. Much soul-searching, arguing, and couples therapy helped us enormously. I did not fall head over heels madly in love with Aaron until our fifth wedding anniversary. Studies show that married couples who stick it out report being much happier in their later years.

11. Do Not Say "Let's Do This Again" If You Don't Mean It: There are many ways to end a date without leading somebody on. If you are absolutely sure that you never, ever want to see your blind date again, you can use such parting lines as, "Thank you so much for this lovely evening," "I really enjoyed our chat," or "It was a pleasure to meet you." If you feel put on the spot by the direct question "Will I see you again?" use your fixer-upper as an excuse to squirm out of it, as in, "Sue said she's having a charity benefit next month. I hope to see you there." The only falsehoods that are fair are little white lies you tell to not hurt somebody's feelings. Remem-

ber, what goes around, comes around. So the next time maybe your feelings will be the ones saved.

12. Do Not Take Your Blind Date to Bed: No matter how pleasurable the feelings are, don't go overboard the first night you meet. The initial interaction is for connecting, getting a good look at each other, having a nice preliminary conversation, smiling, and exchanging information—not body fluids. Jumping into the sack too quickly is impulsive, dumb, and dangerous. If you're completely swept off your feet, keep it to kissing, which at least usually doesn't lead to unwanted pregnancy, syphilis, STDs, HIV, and AIDS. Having sex too soon creates a false sense of intimacy that usually dooms the duet from the start.

Phrases That Will Send Any Matchmaker Fleeing

The kind of matchmaker you're courting is hooking you up for fun, for free, and out of the goodness of her heart. Many fixer-uppers, like me, are not courting headaches, hurt feelings, flaming fiascoes, or anyone's failure or humiliation. So we do preliminary interviews with interested singles to screen out who is really ready for a healthy relationship and who is fooling himself. If you want to be immediately eliminated from the pool of all potential love prospects, here are phrases that would make anybody delete you from her mental marriage list:

- Although my last three boyfriends were drug addicts like my father . . .
- My ex-girlfriend is totally selfish and off her rocker, but she's so beautiful I just can't walk away.

- I know he's a liar, cheater, and a jerk, but the sex is so good I just can't . . .

- I know I swore off actresses with eating disorders after that last psycho-scene, but this one is different because . . .

- After that time he drugged me, it was hard to trust him again because . . .

- I need to find someone who has a lot of money, since I . . .

- I know he went back to his wife and kids twice before, but this time . . .

- Though he placed another personal ad while we were dating, I can understand . . .

- I'm never allowed to call my sweetie at home or go over there because . . .

- I can tell my kids hate his guts when he sleeps over, but they don't understand . . .

- She says we should have an open relationship.

- He mentioned he likes threesomes, and since I wanted to please him . . .

- I know it's only been two weeks, but I just loaned her a few thousand to tide her over.

- He didn't mean to hit me. He promised he won't do it again, so I'm giving him another chance.

- He says he'll never get married or have kids, but he doesn't really mean it because . . .

- I'm open to dating someone new now. I'm just letting my ex crash at my place until she straightens out the lawsuit with her landlord.

- I know he's married, but his wife is a total bitch who doesn't understand him.

- I think a man should pay for everything in the relationship. So the minute I get engaged, I plan to quit
  my job.
- I can't help it, I just can't go out with someone who
  isn't as beautiful and thin as my ex.

12

IF YOU'RE DYING TO
WED TOMORROW

Marriage is a serious bond that should not be jumped into or taken lightly. Yet I admit that every once in a while somebody will present a convincing reason to say "I do" pronto. Ellen, a fifty-six-year-old Manhattan woman who'd never been wed, told me that she'd been angry and depressed when the live-in artist she'd supported for the last decade left her. Two months after they'd split he'd married a younger, richer woman. After the attacks of September 11, 2001, Ellen met an older, widowed businessman—not at all her usual type— who started talking marriage after five months. He was clearly a good, honest man who was very close to his three children. She confessed that although she was merely "fond of him" and not madly in love, she was tempted to elope.

When I asked her to share her reasoning, Ellen said she felt safe with her suitor, was ready to take a risk and do something different, and that at the end of her life she would rather her obituary say she was divorced than never been married. Those are not the worst reasons in the world for tying the knot. In fact, they seemed more rational and sustainable than the common over-the-top reasons to wed, such as "She's the love of my life," "I know I'll never feel this way about someone else as long as I live," and, "I just know I could never live without him."

I would never recommend that someone healthy in his or her twenties or early thirties throw caution to the wind and wed just for the hell of it. If you're not careful, you could wind up swindled, heartbroken, or humiliated. And of course lack of money, revenge, medical problems, close proximity to death and fearing a boring obit, and the end of your family lineage aren't the best or most poetic motivations for fast marriage or parenthood. Yet who says those reasons are any less real or important than the more typical and irrational romantic enticements? Sometimes radical measures are liberating. So for extreme situations, I'm offering some extreme, albeit semisafe, strategies for those who are sick of their singlehood and just want that damn band on their ring finger already.

Do a Major Makeover: I am not usually an advocate of obsessing about your looks or getting cosmetic surgery. But the reality is that for many people, physical attraction in a mate is essential. If you are obese, and having your stomach stapled will help you lose one hundred pounds in six months, you'll probably be much more desirable to the opposite sex. If you've always hated your chest, nose, profile, thighs, dark circles under your eyes, or skin under your chin, then maybe you should go ahead and get that boob, nose, or chin job, lipo, nip, or tuck you've always wanted. Sometimes the difference in how you feel is enough to justify the cost of the reconstruction.

If you can't handle going under the knife, consider Botox, skin peels, manicures, pedicures, hair dye, personal stylists picking out new wardrobes, and nutritionists and personal trainers who'll revamp your menu and workout schedule tomorrow. So if you're a bland and chubby brunette gal with glasses, go blond, buff, and get contact lenses and midnight-red lipstick. If you're broke or too busy working, you can still easily change your clothes, makeup, glasses, or hairstyle.

Sexing up my look worked for me. Although I preferred being lazy in comfortable sweatpants, baggy black jeans, T-shirts, sneakers, or cowboy boots, I forced myself to wake up and makeup. When I really felt ready to find a husband, I joined a gym, started working out, and switched to miniskirts, halter tops, low-cut dresses, high-heeled sandals, and bright red lipstick. It worked. I found a great husband, and a runner-up. (Addendum: I'm currently wearing old sweats, a T-shirt, and no makeup, though I may put on some rouge or lip gloss before my husband comes home.)

Get Rid of Background Barriers: Kim, a great-looking black woman I know, was determined to find an African American man. When she expanded her search to anybody great, she met her spouse—who happened to be white. This was the subject of the hit film *Something New*. The movie's star, Sanaa Lathan, recently told Oprah that the film was inspired by statistics that showed 42 percent of black women in this country don't marry, and that 11 percent of black men date interracially, while only 6 percent of black women do. Being more open to different kinds of dates could bridge that gap. Oprah endorsed the concept, calling it "going global."

I've also seen many successful unions with couples from different religious and ethnic persuasions. My friend Lara, who comes from a conservative Jewish family, had a hard time clicking with men from her tribe. Then she met Glenn, a terrific warm guy whose family happens to be Arab American. You know what? Lara's parents got over it and taught

Glenn's family the hora at their wedding, and both sets of grandparents adore their new granddaughter. I know two Jewish women who followed their hearts and wound up happily married to Chinese men. At my cousin Karin's wedding, her father even made a lovely speech about how Jewish and Chinese cultures both focus on education, family, and food, and thus have much in common. The more color-blind you are, the more chances you have to find a fantastic mate.

Get Over Just One Beauty Block: Many singles say they don't want to date someone who is too short, too tall, bald, has a beard or mustache, is chubby, too skinny, flat chested, gray haired, bowlegged, or disabled. But as an experiment, loosen up and cross one of your long-term taboos off of your physical fantasy list. Face your fear. In fact, revel in it! I'm five feet seven and had always insisted on men over six feet tall. But I made myself agree to go out with any guy who asked, regardless of his height. You know what—it didn't hurt. I actually enjoyed having many more prospects, including one five-foot-seven musician I dated for a year. Turned out it was easier to get around town in flat shoes, and I bought him cowboy boots for his birthday, which made him five feet ten.

When I started getting serious with Aaron, it bothered me that he ate junk food and refused to exercise. But one night at a party I watched a famous, charming, albeit overweight, actor walk in with his luminous, tiny, blond wife. He clearly adored and doted on his mate, who looked like the happiest woman in the room. I heard that he was a great husband and father to their four kids. It occurred to me if I could just get over my superficial stigma about weight—as she had—I could get what I wanted: love and marriage. So I did get over it and married my big guy—who then lost seventy pounds! Every time you can overcome one of your superficial, self-imposed barriers, a thousand more choices will open up before your eyes. And some of the barriers might be more workable later on than you thought.

Females Have Finances Too: Many well-off women I know who are in their forties, fifties, and older insist that someone they date must be financially successful. They don't want to treat, and think going dutch or splitting expenses is an insult. So they don't date. They sit alone in their chic clothes and fancy houses, complaining that men only want twenty-year-old models and that all the good ones are taken. This is silly and small-minded. Everyone has different talents, and quite often men who are not type-A CEOs are better in bed, handier around the house, or more sensitive and nurturing. Marrying a man for money is risky anyway, since more than a few tycoons have been known to have affairs, trade in the old model for trophy wives, lose their fortunes, or end up in jail. So why not take turns paying the bill? Or if a guy you meet seems nice but broke, offer to cook him dinner. Or take him to a movie or a concert. If you fear he might be just dating you for your dollars, suggest inexpensive outings, like taking a walk or going to the zoo. You can mention early on that you're leaving all your money to charity, and that you are a strong believer in prenuptial agreements.

Valerie, my own fixer-upper, smartly chose love over lucre. Although she was a successful filmmaker and Tom, whom she called "her fling," was an out-of-work actor who couldn't afford an engagement ring, she went for it anyway. She paid for the wedding and the honeymoon, and they moved into her apartment, where she paid most of the rent. Here's the rub. Eight years later, her film career was in the toilet and Tom had hit his stride with a new trade. That New Year's he handed her the gorgeous diamond ring he could finally afford and said, "Let's get engaged." She said yes!

Defang Divorce: A lot of solo players say they won't get married if they are not 100 percent sure it will last forever. Some come from divorced homes and don't want to repeat the mistake. Others come from clans so intact they're petrified they'll shame their family if they don't live up to their parents' eternal bond. Too much pressure will doom any partnership, so loosen up. You can't be 100 percent sure of anything, you can't live your life to please your relatives, and you can't make decisions based on fixing your parents' past mistakes. Of course you want your legal link to last forever, but there is no way to assure a union will last. Sometimes it's a crapshoot. If your marriage does not work out, it does not have to leave a lasting scar or stigma. Almost half of marriages in this country fail, but not all divorces have to be ugly and hideous. My girlfriend Lilly stayed close friends with her ex and says she'll never regret her marriage because it gave her the best thing in her life: her two children. Tamara, a journalism student of mine, just wrote a lovely essay about how, when her mother was dying in the South, her former husband surprised her by rushing to the hospital to take care of his former mother-in-law. Instead of resenting it, as Tamara thought she would, she felt so relieved and blessed that it reminded her of the love they'd shared. You don't have to judge a relationship solely by the result.

If you are worried that a breakup could ruin you financially, take steps to protect yourself with a prenuptial agreement, save money in a trust for relatives or friends, and get separate bank accounts and credit cards. You can keep your old apartment as your office, with only your name on the lease and contract. Remember, if you are too afraid of failure, you'll never succeed.

Reconsider the Need to Feel "Madly in Love This Second": If you are twenty years old, I'd recommend holding on to your unrealistic notions of love and passion for a few years longer and see if it works for you. At least until you can go for a few fantasy lovers, have your heart shattered, and get wiser. But if you are past forty, have always wanted to get married, but have never found someone who makes your heart go pitter-patter, you might have seen too many movies that imply your heart should instantly go pitter-patter. Maybe someone's continual sweetness and devotion will cause a stronger and deeper pitter-patter a few years later (as was the case in my marriage).

Many of us have misconceptions and distorted expectations about what the look and definition of "true love" really is. If there is someone in your world whom you love to look at and sleep with, but otherwise find mean, stupid, selfish, unreliable, unstable, or dishonest, run the other way. This isn't true love, it's lust mixed with true masochism. It shocks me how many single people I know who hold on to and use pathetic former relationships as a way to avoid acceptable suitors. They actually cheat themselves out of love that would wind up truer and last forever, if they could just give it a chance.

My dear friend Rachel, a pretty, smart, forty-four-year-old woman who has never been married, keeps comparing Spencer, her most recent sweet suitor, to Karl, her ex-boyfriend. Karl was a depressed, broke alcoholic who could not make a commitment to her during the four years she tried to save him. Everyone who cares about Rachel recalls her saying she was madly in love with Karl but wishes she would marry Spencer, despite the fact that she says she only feels "safe, protected" and "a mild pleasure" when she's with him. I argue that it's much better to feel "protected" and "mild pleasure" with a winner who wants you than to stay madly in love with an impossible loser who doesn't. Plus what you feel today isn't necessarily all there is. Love can expand and grow in wonderful ways with time and commitment. Rachel argues that she's better off single than being with Spencer out of default and doesn't want to settle.

In some ways, making any choice could be thought of as settling, and the word does not deserve its bad reputation. If waiting around for some ridiculous fantasy that's never going to happen is what you call "chasing your dream," then sometimes "settling" is a smarter plan of action. Apply this logic to other arenas in your life. Yes, it would be nice to live in a marble-filled mansion with a tennis court and swimming pool. But renting or buying a small starter house within your budget and then fixing it up can bring more satisfaction and comfort because you created your own special home. Is it "settling" to live somewhere you can afford? How many of us take internships or lower-level jobs, then work our way up the ladder to our targeted position? Is it "settling" to get rid of your sense of entitlement, be realistic, and work hard? If most of us sat home hoping to be called to interview for the perfect position, we'd probably spend our lives unemployed and living off our parents. Waiting too long, or expecting your dream to fall into your lap, can be both self-sabotaging and self-destructive.

If Rachel was younger, adored her career and social life, hadn't followed this pattern ten times before, and didn't keep saying how lonely, broke, frustrating, and horrible being alone is, I might cut her more slack and say "hold out for true love." But at forty-four, she's been dating for thirty years and has never felt "true love" for anybody capable of loving her back. So right now my money is on Spencer. Rachel's therapist agrees and they are working on why it's so hard for Rachel to fall for someone kind and healthy.

Also consider this: many single people have an inaccurate sense of what they are currently capable of feeling. I know several talented artists and interesting, complex, type-A workaholics who have narcissistic, depressive, addictive, or manic personality types. They might function extremely well at work, or with friends. But when it comes to romance, they always feel that the lover they are with is somehow not good enough, and that somebody better will come along. I always remember my shrink Dr. Woolverton's mantra: *feelings misinform*. Just because you feel it, doesn't mean it's accurate, true, or makes any sense. You can learn to stop acting on irrational emotions and stop repeating self-defeating patterns. It's possible to understand your limitations, make a commitment to somebody good, and fight the part of you that has led you astray before. The process begins by listening to your trusted advisers and following your brain but not your heart.

If you are lucky enough to find somebody who is smart, warm, and good, whom you care about deeply, are immensely fond of, enjoy spending time with, feel protected by, and want to take care of, consider making it legal. Focus on the really important stuff—like if this person is generous and kind to you and your parents, siblings, and children. Use my friend Annie's question as your criterion: if I were in the hospital, would he come to see me every day and bring me flowers?

If this is what you consider settling, then it's time to nix the colloquial definition that implies it's accepting a subpar romantic relationship. Let's now link the word to "settling up one's affairs," which, according to *Webster's*, means "to appoint, fix, or resolve definitely and conclusively," and "to place in a desired state or in order." Settlement is "the state of being settled, the act of making stable or putting on a permanent basis." I am not saying grab on to the closest partner who wants you, marry him, and never leave, even if you are miserable. That's chaotic and irresponsible, the exact opposite of order. I am suggesting that often it's quite healthy to make a rational decision to stop chasing after physical infatuation and unrequited feelings that have hurt you in the past. Instead, you can enhance your life with an adult, positive, real, stable, and binding type of love. There are many different ways to love someone, and often feelings transform and grow deeper after marriage. I loved Aaron when we tied the knot, but I did not really fall deeply and madly in love with him until our fifth anniversary. Now my heart really does go all aflutter when he comes home every night! So maybe, like me, you're the type who will have a delayed reaction.

Go Out with Every Nice Person Who Asks: You're thirty-four years old and she's fifty? So what? She could wind up being brilliant and charming. You're a corporate lawyer and he's a hairdresser who never even finished high school? Maybe it'll do you good to be with someone who doesn't overintellectualize all the time. Force yourself to stop being judgmental, superficial, ageist, and limited. This method—even for a short time—will introduce you to new friends of different backgrounds, and help you brush up on your social skills. If you're open to all the nice people who cross your path, and are willing to be surprised, it could lead you to a better, more real kind of love than you expected. That was the case for Maria Dahvana Headley, a twenty-year-old single NYU student who feared she was too critical of men. So for a year she dated anybody decent who asked her out. The result was her funny book *The Year of Yes*, and her marriage—to an older divorced playwright whom in the past she would have easily dismissed.

Go Back to the Future: Think back to the relationship in your past that made you the happiest. Between Google, your alumni association, and old friends, it usually is not all that difficult to find out if that person is married, or single and available. If your onetime sweetheart is not married, send an e-mail, brief note, or leave a phone message just to say hello. If your ex is interested in reconnecting, ask to meet for a casual cup of coffee—even if you have to fake a family trip to his neck of the woods or show up at the next school reunion. It might just turn out as wonderful as the experience of my new friend Michelle Mead, who at fifty-five is newly engaged to her college boyfriend, John Armor.

Similarly, TV/radio reporter Donna Hanover married the handsome ex-boyfriend who had broken her heart in college and wrote the charming book *My Boyfriend's Back* about it. If the love of your former life turns out to be married, gay, on drugs, in jail, or no longer the least bit interested in you, check out your number two. Or three. Keep going down the list. Why should you look back at people who broke your heart before? Because most people are a hell of a lot smarter at forty or fifty-five than at fifteen or twenty-five. Plus there is sometimes a trust and comfort level with somebody you used to know back when.

Atone for Past Relationship Sins: While you're robbing your own romantic history, write a list of all the hearts you broke and feelings you hurt when you were younger. Then make a plan to make contact. Especially with the nice ones you blew off out of youthful idiocy, superficiality, or stupidity. You can emulate the main character in the TV hit *My Name Is Earl*, who is asking everyone he ever screwed over, lied to, or cheated for forgiveness. Write a lovely e-mail, letter, or card along the lines of "I have been thinking about all the stupid things I did in my past, and recall that many moons ago, I did not treat you nicely. I hope you'll accept my apology and wishes that all is well." Make sure to put your home address, phone number, and e-mail in case he wants to respond to you. If he does, offer to buy your ex breakfast, lunch, dinner, or coffee. Travel to his town for this meeting. Maybe you'll find that the person is single and has aged well and grown more attractive to you. At this point you're more realistic and more desperate, but a little bit of desperation can be a good motivator. And here's the best trick about old lovers: sometimes their eyes see you the same as you were when you first met.

13

WHEN IT'S BETTER
TO MARRY LATER

I know getting married at twenty-three years old is a new trend. It's often followed by an old trend: divorce. Everyone is different and only you can judge your emotional maturity. I am sure there are some singles who have fixed up themselves and their lives enough to pass the Ready-for-True-Romance test by age twenty-three. But you must gauge your readiness, your selfishness, and your goals in life. If, like my high school friend Joanie, your deepest desire is to be a great mother to six children, marrying young and getting pregnant in your early twenties (like she did) seems like good sense.

On the other hand, in *Letters to a Young Poet*, Rainer Maria Rilke suggested that certain people with poetic sensibilities (like writers and artists who don't want to follow the typical path) should wait until they are at least thirty-five to settle down with a soul mate. That was true in my case, and I found my midthirties to be the ideal time to combine my life, apartment, bank account, and books with another's. Had I waited many more years, I might have become bored or bitter. But had I tried it earlier, chances are it would not have lasted because I wasn't ready. I needed to get myself, my career, and my psyche together first.

Quite often, when it comes up in conversation that my sideline is matchmaking, singles I meet say, "I would love to meet somebody, but I'm too old to be fixed up." Then they add, "I'm thirty-eight." Or, "I'm in my forties." Or fifties, or sixties, or seventies. Although the ages of my fix-ups have ranged from eighteen to ninety, I actually prefer to fix up pairs who are middle-aged or older. They know who they are. They have less time to waste on silly or superficial matters. They appreciate a good match when they see it and don't mince words or actions.

My childhood friends in the Midwest started tying the knot at nineteen. Some of them had been double knotted by twenty-five. One thirty-six-year-old vixen I know has just sworn to her third set of vows. But I'm glad I waited until thirty-five to do it for the first time, and that Aaron, who is eleven years older than I, took his initial walk down the aisle at age forty-six, with salt-and-pepper hair and laugh lines under the eyes. I would not necessarily suggest waiting for Social Security, but there are many benefits of marrying later:

1. Shock Value: People are so surprised that you're finally doing it at last that everyone shows up and makes a much bigger deal about your wedding. Long-forgotten acquaintances and distant relatives you didn't even invite send cards, checks, and crystal vases.

2. No Midlife Marriage Crisis: You're already in midlife! You never thought it would happen, so you are filled with glee, grace, and gratitude. If you're lucky, by the time the novelty wears off, you're dead.

3. Moneybags: In middle age, your midriff has grown, but so has your bank account. Nothing jump-starts a new life together like two bathrooms, enough closet space, and the occasional first-class hotel on an expense account. Teenagers often think sleeping on the floor of a dirty European youth hostel is romantic. As a middle ager, five-star hotels are usually much more of an aphrodisiac. Don't underestimate the benefits of physical comfort.

4. Swinging Single: Remember all those illusions about the glamorous time you would have alone? Well, you played it out. Being a slob, wearing sweatpants all day, eating cold pizza for breakfast, and not answering to anyone pales beside having a built-in warm body for a Saturday-night movie date.

5. Hope Chest: All your competitive and unmarried friends in their forties, fifties, and sixties flock around, buoyed by your sudden switch in marital status. They say things like, "You were the last person I ever thought I would see walk down the aisle," and, "If you could do it, anybody can." Take it as a compliment and talk often and openly about how wonderful it is to find love a little on the later side. It's nice to give others inspiration!

6. Fountain of Youth: When reminiscing with your partner, you can exaggerate or have selective memories about your youthful days—since they were so long before you met. "I was so skinny in college," "I used to dress much more provocatively," or "I was so much more popular with the opposite sex back then," adds to the myth and the mystery. Thank goodness all your lovely but loser exes are locked away in photograph albums.

7. You Are Secure with Your Insecurities: You've been there, done that, and screwed it up so many times that you don't even have to bother hiding your sordid fears. At a certain age, jealousy and vanity actually seem cute.

8. Technophilia: Combining long lives usually involves upgrading technology, since chances are one of you has already acquired a decent CD player, television, DVD player, fax, laptop, laser printer, iPod, cell phone, BlackBerry, TiVo, and top-of-the-line blow dryer.

9. Therapy Pays Off: All that time and money spent in psychoanalysis, Alcoholics Anonymous, transactional analysis, est, and Gestalt, watching Oprah and Dr. Phil, and taking yoga, Pilates, and meditation classes has clearly sunk into your system. When steamed or upset, you now know how to say, "I think I'll go take a walk to cool off, so I don't kill you," "Perhaps we shouldn't bring seven years of hostility into an argument about a toaster oven," or, "I'm going to make a shrink appointment now."

10. War Stories: You've been around the block. Did it in an elevator. A plane bathroom. The beach. This led to a sprained ankle, angry passengers hopping up and down, and sand in your shoes for six months after the passion ended. You've finally learned it's much more comfortable with someone you love. In a bed. Lying down.

14

HOW TO CLOSE THE DEAL

Once you get involved with someone special, there are several turns the relationship can take, ranging from eternal adoration to endless indecision to devastating heartbreak. If you are sure that you want your sweetie to become your spouse, there are ways to get rolling and glide down the aisle. Conversely, there are ways to completely screw it up and wind up broke, broken up, divorced, furious, and desperately regretting your actions forever. Here are some hints to making your love both legally binding and lasting.

Four Months Is Usually Too Soon: From all of my experiences and research, I'd say that the appropriate, average time to start thinking about marrying someone is after you've been dating about a year. Perhaps if your partner is a childhood friend of your family, or if you first dated in high school (and found this person to be honest and earnest), you could get away with a shorter courtship. There are sometimes other compelling reasons to rush. If you are a never-married forty-year-old currently pregnant with twins, it's understandable that you wouldn't want to draw out the engagement. But tread carefully. Better your children be born out of wedlock than you wind up rushing into something with a person who could hurt, swindle, or deceive you. I know, we all hear lovely stories of star-crossed lovers who eloped after four dates. They often end up like Renée Zellweger and Kenny Chesney, who fell in love at first sight, married four months later in May, and had an annulment by the fall. This is your life you're talking about. Your public records, material wealth, family, future offspring, and reputation are at stake. It'll probably take at least twelve months to make sure that what you see is really what you're getting.

Four Years Is Usually Too Long: Unless you met in college and are now twenty-six, or both mutually agreed to wait until you finish graduate degrees or can afford to buy a house, unending courtships tend to be boring and bad news. If you are sure you're ready for matrimony and your mate isn't, move on with your life alone. Waiting around for somebody you love to decide if you're good enough to marry is never a place you want to stay very long. Plus when *you* end a romance, it's much easier to meet somebody new. Not to mention that jealousy could wake up your old suitor fast.

When in Doubt, Keep Dating: I know many people think that the minute you start getting serious with someone, you should automatically stop meeting and being friendly with other potential suitors. Not me! Okay, if your relationship is soaring along at the perfect speed and within a year you're engaged, then you have no need to keep your eyes open. But in my case, getting my commitment-phobe to propose involved an agonizing six-year-off-and-on-again courtship. By then I wasn't sure Aaron was ever going to come through. So the day he put the diamond ring on my finger was the day that I stopped seeing other men. Okay, I wasn't bed hopping or going to bars every night to check out the scenery. But I was working on my career and my life, going out to fun dancing parties with whichever friends I wanted, and kept going on blind lunch and coffee dates. While I'd only recommend rampant screwing around to someone who wants an STD or early death, dancing around and lunching around are a different story. I've found that being busy, popular, and sought after is the perfect aphrodisiac to hurry up a reluctant suitor. It's certainly much more fun, pride-inducing, proactive, and attractive than pathetically waiting for the phone to ring while moaning that your love isn't sure he wants to marry you.

Don't Be Deceptive: Don't tell someone you are seeing that you are completely committed to him and then renew your subscription to J-Date or Match.com. Even if you just want to see if anybody responds for the fun of it. You will get caught and he will forever tell everyone you know in common that you are a cheater and a liar. Be honest—or at least be elusive. If your love asks where you are going Saturday night, tell the truth and answer, "To the movies," "Out with friends," "Out to dinner," or "To a party." You don't have to cough up whom you are going with. If your potential mate persists, you can say, "I care about you, but I'm not convinced this is it." Then tell him why and give him a chance to convince you.

Don't Cohabitate Before Saying I Do: Sorry, but until you are engaged to be married, sharing your house, money, and all aspects of your day-to-day life isn't a great idea. It can be very aggravating to reside with someone you're hoping will propose but doesn't. You don't want to be a pest, but every minute can remind you of what you don't have. If you argue about it, you don't even have the power to leave—you could be stuck in your own home, wallowing for years with someone who can't come through for you. While you're shacking up, it's virtually impossible to meet anybody else and most of the people you'll come across—from your mailman, to your neighbors and newspaper carrier—will know you are taken and unavailable but also ringless. So they won't ask you out or invite you to events or parties. On the other hand, keeping your own place can add to the mystery and momentum of a relationship. Not being available every day and night to your partner gives both men and women the incentive to get closer by making it official.

I tried to live with someone twice before I met Aaron. Both times I wound up feeling like I had all the responsibilities of a spouse without any of the perks (including the ring, reception, status, legal protection, and the family respect). I know you have to take a risk with romance. But sharing your heart and body is enough of a risk; you don't have to share your lease. Studies show that couples who cohabited before marriage divorce just as often as couples who haven't. If you're lonely, get a roommate, a cat, or a puppy. If you're broke and totally dig the idea of sharing your date's hot real estate, go back to Chapter 2 and learn how to Fix Up Yourself First.

Don't Wait for a Wedding to Promote Yourself: I know you always pictured making major decisions, purchases, and investments with your significant other beside you. But if the person you are dating isn't stepping up to the plate, then she is forfeiting her right to an opinion about how you live. If you want and can afford to buy yourself a better home, fancy furniture, a new car, a boat, jewelry, or art, or take an exotic vacation, do not wait until your partner proposes before you treat yourself to luxury. If you earned it, you have a right to spend and enjoy it. And anyway, your partner—along with other people of the opposite sex—will be much more attracted to someone living it up than someone waiting at home for the phone to ring.

Make Room for Two of Everything Everywhere: Although I don't suggest handing the keys to your apartment to someone you are dating, it's still good practice to rearrange your living quarters so there's space for two people. Even if you are not dating anybody special at the moment, consider buying a queen- or king-size bed, keep a drawer or hangers in your closet empty so some hypothetical someone could someday leave clothes at your place, put an extra new toothbrush in the holder in the bathroom, and get rid of gender-specific bedroom decorations (like pink teddy bears or football regalia) so that a potential lover might feel more at home.

When you do find someone special enough to bring home, these details might make him visualize how warm and wonderful it could be being married to a nurturing person who cares about his comfort and literally has room for him, along with whetting his appetite for more closeness. I still remember how sweet it was to visit Aaron's apartment in L.A. and find a picture of us together up on his bulletin board. Even if he just tacked it up there a few minutes before I arrived to make me feel special—it worked! Feng shui practices even suggest having everything in your place in pairs—like two turtle doves—to spiritually ready yourself for sharing love.

Hang Out with the Happily Married: There is nothing more inspiring than being around pairs who've said "I do" and keep doing it passionately. Although double dating with "smug marrieds" right away may be pushing it, after you and your partner have reached the three-month mark, seek out those joyously wed—of all ages. They will teach you how to do it, look out for your best interests, and let you know when somebody you love, or think you might love, is not marriage material. When I was single, spending time with my cousins Howard and Bette Fast, an adorable duet who were forty years older than me, was a blessing. I brought around all of my boyfriends to get Howard and Bette's opinion. They nixed several of my suitors out of hand (and turned out to be right on each account). Interestingly, after meeting Aaron the first time, Bette called my mother and said, "He's a mensch. She's going to marry this one." Bette passed away not long after. But she was on the money and I've always been so grateful that Aaron met her and had her approval.

Avoid Bitter Divorcés: I know half of marriages end in divorce and I don't discriminate over who I spend time with when I'm alone. But when it comes to socializing, I would never subject brand-new suitors to those in the middle of bad breakups or divorces. Even though we've been married for ten years, I've also tried to steer Aaron clear of friends who are in the midst of ugly splits. When Les, whose divorce was just finalized, asked Aaron to go to Mexico with him, I put my foot down. This was after I had a two-hour conversation with Les, who disagreed with my motto "It takes two not to tango." Instead he irrationally argued that his ex of twenty-five years was to blame for everything that had gone wrong in his marriage. Our talk was disheartening, and reinforced my belief that angry breakup energy can be toxic.

I've suggested to my divorcing friends that we go to movies, theater, or big crowded parties, hoping fun spectacles would distract them from their sorrow. When one sad ex-spouse said she couldn't yet handle being in public, I kept connected to her by e-mail, snail mail, or phone. Other people's joy, frustration, or pain can rub off on you. Unless it's your parent, child, or sibling—or you work as a therapist—it's healthier to limit the hours you spend on other people's crisis management. You'll be better off hanging around with people you want to be like. If you're trying to get hitched, spending time with happy pairs will make it easier to emulate them.

Keep Your Big Mouth Shut: Your lover does not have to know how many previous sex partners you've had, whether you ever tried a threesome or anal sex, how many abortions you've undergone or caused, every drug you consumed in college, all the addictions and mental illness in your extended family, or what your exact wedding fantasy is. Not now, not upon the eve of your engagement, maybe not ever. In fact, if you want there to be an engagement and wedding, tread carefully with secrets and don't supply too much unnecessary and irrelevant information. I'm not saying that you should lie. But no matter how many times Aaron asks, I will not tell him the number of men I slept with before him. No matter how many times I ask, he will not show me pictures of his old girlfriends or letters they wrote him. Some things are private, and should remain so forever. If you must blab, this is what best buddies, shrinks, and therapy groups were invented for.

Keep Your Family Out of It: For some people, introducing their beloved to their parents constitutes seriousness. But beware of getting the family involved too soon or too often, especially if there's a history of dysfunction on either side. There are many ways an intrusive or inappropriate clan can destroy your romance. One dad I know, a wealthy banker, prematurely mentioned that any bride his son Sam wed would have to sign a prenuptial agreement. Sam's girlfriend disagreed and—even before they were ready to talk about marriage—this issue broke them up. Tony, a white student of mine, brought home Shirley, his black girlfriend, after two months of dating. Tony's mother disapproved of their differences, which made Tony rebel and want to see her more. You never want to date someone for rebellion or to make a political statement. This started a complicated domestic drama that ended with Tony and his mother not speaking to each other.

Your family could like someone you're courting too much and start calling her, inviting her over, or buying her presents before you've decided if she is the one. Be especially careful when you are considering introducing your date to your children. A few toys or Gummi Bears and kids can glob on to someone fast. If they've already been through a parent's death or divorce, do you want them to get close to someone who might not stick around that long? I wouldn't meet someone's children until it's clear you want to audition for the role of stepparent. If you can't even imagine playing that part, then what the hell are you doing buying toys and Gummi Bears? Do you really want to lead on and then crush the heart of a young child as well as his parent?

If you fear that throwing everyone together over a holiday could get uncomfortable, make plans beforehand to avoid confusion and discomfort. Consider sharing just the meal, or dessert and drinks later, rather than spending an entire day together. Discuss whether you would prefer to be introduced as "my friend," "my girlfriend," "my partner," or another term, so nobody's feelings will be hurt. Only accept invitations from your date, and not his mother, sister, or children. Don't make assumptions about who is close to whom in a family you are just meeting. Some people have long-term feuds going with their parents or siblings and you don't want to unwittingly get caught in the cross fire.

Make ground rules about what feels appropriate for both parties in a relationship. Beth, a woman I know, started receiving late-night phone calls from her divorced boyfriend Brian's ten-year-old daughter. When her boyfriend didn't approve of the connection, Beth argued. She was wrong. Turned out she fell more in love with Brian's kids than with him, and this created another awkward breakup that hurt everyone more than it had to. Sometimes it's best to keep it short and casual with your partner's clan until the wedding—when all domestic hell will break out anyway.

Don't Fear Weirdness and Discomfort: Everyone has wistful Hollywood images of how wonderful true love, courtship, engagement, wedding, honeymoon, and newlywed days are. Forget it! My courtship with Aaron was often awkward and agonizing. At times he did anything he could think of to avoid getting too close, including not calling me for two weeks at a time. I broke up with him and started dating other guys so often that when I called my parents to finally tell them I was engaged, they said, "To whom?" The ring Aaron picked out was too tight and made my finger turn red and swell. I gained ten pounds and felt lethargic and out of it during my entire engagement. My sister-in-law had the first grandchild of the family on the day of my wedding, which I spent feeling confused and resentful. I was too tired to have sex that night anyway. Our Jamaica honeymoon wasn't all that romantic either. I hated the hotel we picked, and we continually argued over my smoking in the room.

I was jealous when my friend Gayle chronicled her wonderful scenic outdoor wedding and how she and her husband, Nick, made ecstatic love for hours after their reception. Gayle and Nick divorced after two years, while Aaron and I are stronger ten years later. Everyone is different. Keep your expectations in check. That way, if certain stages are painful, you're prepared and won't overreact, take it as a bad omen, and run away. And if things turn out to be pretty and passionate after all, you'll be pleasantly surprised.

15

LOVE AND MARRIAGE
MYTHS TO LOSE

I was quite startled and offended years ago when my therapist, Dr. Gross, told me that "everything you've ever thought
about love and marriage is wrong." Yet the longer I'm wed
and the more couples I weld, the clearer it becomes that almost all single people have major misconceptions about
dating and mating. It's easy to analyze the sources and under-
lying motivations for all the phoniness and false advertising.
Unfortunately, blaming Hollywood, Broadway musicals, romance novels, political propaganda, religious dogma, or your
parents' desperation for grandchildren will not switch your
marital status. What's more important is that you realize how
these misperceptions can keep you from getting the spouse
you keep saying you want. Here are the fiction and fantasies
you are holding on to that hurt your chances for finding a satisfying real-life partner.

It Should Be Love at First Sight: In actuality, if both
members of a new couple say they have "great chemistry"

or feel an intense physical attraction right away, I get worried and assume it won't last. If somebody uses the *L* word or the *M* word within a few weeks, I fear the relationship is doomed. By starting with wildly romantic, unrealistic expectations, there is usually nowhere else to go but to disappointment. In my experience, if someone calls me to say the fix-up "seemed nice" and might be worth one more try for the hell of it, that connection stands a much better chance of catching fire in the future.

I Have a Type: I recall the male friend of a friend who said he preferred tall, thin, waify actresses decades his junior. That wasn't his "type." It was his vice, superficial obsession, and limitation in life. No wonder he was fifty-seven years old, lonely, single, and seen by many in his social circle as a ridiculous lecher. I guessed that keeping these requirements was a way for Peter Pan to keep his fears of intimacy at bay. A forty-four-year-old girlfriend of mine still gravitates toward handsome, self-involved, suffering artists in leather jackets and on motorcycles, despite having been hurt by this type multiple times over the years. She recently mentioned, with disdain, that a new date was nerdy, albeit very nice, and became mad at me when I suggested she should get together with Mr. Nice again. "So I should go out with anybody with a penis who is straight and nice?" she asked me. "Yes! Exactly!" I answered. "A straight guy who is nice, and interested in you—why don't you make that your new type?" Get rid of your type and you might find a real person.

I Want Love, So I'm Ready for Love: When guests I meet at parties hear that I'm a fix-up fanatic, they often want me to set them up. In asking them specific questions about themselves, they tend to chain-smoke, get drunk, get high, or overeat while trashing their families, friends, bosses, fellow partygoers, or their host (without asking if I am close with the host or the people we are standing near). When I inquire why they are single, I hear many hostile stories about monster exes and clichés about the opposite sex ("All women really want sugar daddies," or, "All the good men are already taken"). Don't people hear what they sound like? Can't they tell how their rage has already programmed the outcome of the social event? These displays are fascinating for a student of human behavior, but I can often only recommend a date with a therapist.

I Should Be Swept Off My Feet: Perhaps everyone has the escapist fantasy that someone regal will waltz her off to a magical island far away from reality's day-to-day demands and disappointments. But the moment you feel swept off your feet is exactly when you should start worrying and look for a parachute. If something seems too good to be true, assume it is. And if you can't wait to throw away the life you've created for yourself, you need to go back and create a better one. Your goal should be to find a mate while keeping your feet firmly planted on the ground.

I Have to Trust My Heart: It sounds sincere and earnest, but the truth is: your heart can easily lead you to hell in a handbag. Most of our feelings and heartfelt notions have been formed and informed by our childhood. So we instinctively gravitate toward what we already know. If Daddy was an abusive alcoholic, the chances are you are going to feel true love for an abusive alcoholic. If Mom was a doormat who subjugated her own needs, that's what you'll do in a heartbeat. Your heart will often go out to somebody needy who is in trouble. But being a caretaker can be boring and counterproductive, as is repeating your parents' relationship. Stop listening to Hallmark's misleading messages. Instead, gather and study statistics from experts and believe what your brain is telling you. Or trust the Yiddish proverb "The heart is half a prophet" and commingle the two.

I Have to Trust My Gut: People overuse this expression to imply that the first fast impulse one has is often right. Despite the high sales numbers of Malcolm Gladwell's book *Blink*, I don't think that concept holds water when it comes to marriage. (Isn't Gladwell still single?) Our initial instincts often lead us astray. Just look at your first cool haircut, groovy outfit, or new car. (Red Trans Am anyone?) Was the first major you picked in college the one you stuck with? Were the initial friendships you formed always with the right people? Was your earliest job the one that lasted longest? Haven't you ever bought something you loved, only to return it later when you realized you didn't want/need/love it as much as you thought you did when you saw it at the store or on the Web site? Many personalities should never act on their unguarded desires and would be better off fighting against all of their most basic emotions. If not, someone depressed might hurt himself. Someone shy would hide in her house and never go out. Someone manic might invest every cent she has in the scheme of the moment. Instead of making rash decisions or rushing love, in some cases it's better to trust your family, friends, advisers, and past experiences.

A Good Relationship Is Effortless: A single friend recently commented on how sweet, easy, and contented my husband and I seem together. "It only took years of almost killing each other to look so blissful," I joked. But I wasn't really joking. I've never known a happy couple without conflicts. Freud said there are two life forces—work and love. Many of us toil for decades to get our jobs and careers together, yet are ready to give up on a potential love match in mere weeks, for dumb reasons. Anything good is worth fighting for—and fighting through.

The Beginning Is the Best Part: I know you're picturing flowers, candy, red hearts, champagne, and long walks arm-in-arm. But sometimes courtships are chaotic and confusing. Moving in together and tying the knot can be agonizing, especially if you are not spring chickens when you unite. Merging separate lives, homes, furniture, books, bank accounts, pets, friends, and families can seem unnatural and weird and take a lot of time to adjust to. I found the first five years of marriage to be the hardest. After that, everything became blissful. Now I can't wait to kiss my husband every night when he comes home from work and I miss him when he leaves in the morning. It didn't surprise me when a recent National Center for Health Statistics study showed that couples who stay together the longest are happier and live longer than those who are single and divorced.

My Lover Should Read My Mind: Whether it's during a date, sex, or in the middle of planning your wedding or honeymoon, there is only one person in the universe who knows what is really going on inside that head of yours— and that is you. If you refuse to share that information, then don't expect to ever be understood or get what you want. Conversely, if you do plan to get what you want, the easiest way to do so is to say exactly what that is. Aloud. Clearly. Kindly. And not once or twice but every day, as a matter of course.

Love Will Make Me Happy: Once you have grown out of infanthood, another person will never, ever make you happy in life. Oh sure, a prom date can be fun, a good orgasm can put a smile on your face, and the wedding reception of your dreams can take over your world for a year or two. But then what? We all have to get out of bed in the morning, take a shower, get dressed, and go somewhere alone. You can't exist vicariously through someone else's successes and failures and nobody can live, breathe, feel, or make decisions for you. If you think someone else can, try it. You'll wind up lonely, angry, resentful, and bitter in no time at all. In which case there is only one course of action: look in the mirror and figure out what you need to thrive.

My Mate Should Always Come First: This is not true and is downright dangerous to your day-to-day existence. No matter how much you adore your spouse, you must always put yourself first. If you put someone else's needs and wants before your own, you will become a doormat, constantly subjugating your own needs until you disappear. This is also true with children. To best take care of your child, you have to first be strong and healthy. If an airplane is in trouble and losing altitude, and you put the oxygen mask on your baby first, you could die and cause your baby's death—because your child will have no way to get off the plane. So put the oxygen mask on yourself first. Once you do that, you have a much better chance at saving yourself, your baby, and all the rest of the passengers on the plane. There is no more essential love than self-love. If this sounds selfish to you, spend time around selfless caretaker types. They are often tired, burned out, and resentful. In my experience, successful people who get what they want and need tend to be more humble, tolerant, and kind, and have more to give others.

I Deserve Unconditional Love: Only in childhood will you find anyone who will accept and adore you without conditions. Yet even doting parents, grandparents, and siblings expect certain kinds of decent behavior in return for their affection. There are fair expectations in all social interactions and you never have the right to mistreat a loved one, ignore his needs, or take him for granted.

Right after we were married, my husband yelled at me for the way I was putting away his belongings in our new home. I realized that he was not used to sharing his living space. But no matter how great he was in other areas, and as much as I wanted our marriage to work, this was not acceptable to me and I asked him to calm down. By his third loud and hurtful outburst, I packed my bags and surprised my parents by showing up at their doorstep in Michigan. "We're not getting divorced, he's just being an asshole and I need a break," I told them. Then my husband phoned, apologized, sent me flowers, and sent my mother flowers. After a week relaxing by the pool with old friends and relatives who made me feel cherished, I returned to my marriage. My husband has never irrationally screamed at me for anything else since. You have to teach people how to treat you and my message was clear: if you freak out and yell, act mean, rude, or verbally abusive, I will leave. You only get my love and my literal presence on the condition that you treat me well.

All adult love is conditional. If you can't live up to your end of the bargain, you risk being rejected and alone.

Now That We're Engaged, Everything Will Get Easier: Actually, slipping that pretty ring on your finger could open up Pandora's Box. All of your former sins, hidden addictions, buried fears, exes, creditors, and crazy broke needy relatives could come out of the woodwork. I can't tell you how many brides I know who announced their engagement only to never set a date, or to be left at the altar, or to wind up quickly divorced. Unfortunately you don't know if you'll work out together until you work it out together. So don't quit your job, give up your independence, get rid of your friends, or merge all your bank accounts just yet. In fact, if you don't quit your job, give up your independence, get rid of your friends, or merge all your bank accounts, your marriage will have a much better chance of lasting.

My Wedding Will Be the Most Meaningful Night of My Life: For some lucky couples, their ceremonies and receptions will be wonderful occasions. For the wedding industry, there will be megabucks' worth of silly ice sculptures, overpriced flowers, impractical white gowns and veils that will never be worn again. For some of us, the secret is: they suck. These events often consist of overdressed people from two different clans stuck together during a long sit-down dinner punctuated by Hallmark card speeches, cheesy music, gossip about your old lovers and whether or not you're pregnant, while flashes blind everyone. For this your parents might pay thousands of dollars, or perhaps you'll pay and start your marriage deeply in debt. Throw in long ceremonies, bad toasts, humiliating rituals like shoving cake in your face and forcing single people to try to catch a bouquet, and too much alcohol—and you could have an ugly tribal zoo on your hands. Don't expect to feel like a princess, or moved beyond words, or eternally changed. Sometimes a wedding is just a big, overpriced party. Love is the real prize.

My Honeymoon Will Be the Most Romantic Trip I Ever Take: Some duos travel well together and do have a blast on their first married foray. Others don't do well on exotic journeys. They can get jet lag, food poisoning, and sunburned, and feel claustrophobic cohabitating in a small hotel room far from the comforts and rituals of their home base. I know many newlyweds who've confessed that they were overwhelmed from too many wedding events, drained, and confused, and would have preferred to sleep it off in their own bed for two weeks. The pressure to feel amorous on a full-time basis, look perfect in a bathing suit, please this person who's now in your face all the time, and perform sexually every night can be paralyzing. If this is the case, don't worry, and put it in perspective. It's much better to have a lousy honeymoon and a great marriage than vice versa.

Everyone Will Be So Happy for Me: Not really. When you find The One, single friends might be jealous and afraid that you're deserting them. Widows are understandably mourning their own lost mates. Divorcés are probably depressed about their failure or skeptical of your seemingly joyous union. Your exes, siblings, or children may feel bitter and resentful that they'll lose your affection and attention. Those happily married often fear that you're doing it bigger or better than they did. Your family could be wishing you had wound up with your last love, who they liked better. Do not expect to be treated as the center of the universe. Be happy for yourself.

I Get My Way on My Big Day: I know there's some unwritten rule that those getting hitched get to govern the goings-on. But for your own peace of mind, plan in advance that every code and convention you carefully chose will be broken. You can't control the weather, air, train, and automobile traffic, nor can you manipulate workers and guests to be good and do as you wish. Be assured that someone will show up with a date you weren't expecting, a relative will bring her uninvited baby who will cry or throw up during your ceremony. Someone who RSVP'd yes will be a no-show. If you are serving steak, the escort of a guest you barely know will insist on a vegetarian meal. Just because you said black tie doesn't mean Aunt Marge won't show up in an orange pantsuit or your cousin Ken won't wear a T-shirt under his tux and sneakers. Just leave room for the chaos theory and let it go.

I Should Feel Madly in Love: There are many different definitions of love. Some people can only feel erotically charged by somebody unavailable or unkind and aren't capable of being in love with a healthy person. If your decades-old pattern of following your heart hasn't led you to happiness, it's time to follow your brain. In certain cases, merely caring deeply or feeling real affection for somebody good might be the closest you can get to real love. You do not have to feel madly in love or certain that your partner is the love of your life when you say "I do." Feeling that your mate is a kind, wonderful, smart, honest person you want to feel more for may be enough. Often actions are more important than semantics, and the deeper, more lasting kind of love will develop in time.

I Shouldn't Be Ambivalent: Why not? Intelligent, complex people feel and juggle contradictory emotions all the time. People who are always sure of their decisions tend to be either simpleminded dolts or closed-off blowhards. There are fantastic reasons to get married. But taking vows before God, your love, and your in-laws also means that you can no longer be immature, date around, get drunk and party all night, and wind up in bed with anybody cute whom you want. You have to grow up, get real, compromise, answer to somebody else, and decide if you want to have children or not. It's much better to acknowledge the trade-off and mourn the loss of possibilities than to pretend all is wonderful and lie to yourself. Still, instead of sharing your every minor misgiving with your partner (who might be feeling something else entirely), consider talking it out with your best friend, parent, sibling, a clergy member, or your matchmaker.

Now That We Wed, the Pressure Is Off: While a good marriage can certainly provide a more relaxing comfort zone than being out there in the dating scene, don't get too comfortable in your sweatpants and torn T-shirt. It takes a lot of effort and work to keep a long-term union interesting, honest, and spicy. My husband and I try not to dump our bad moods, chores, and complaints on each other the minute we get home from work. (What could be less sexy than hearing, "Here's why my boss is such a dumb jerk," or, "Why didn't you get more toilet paper?" from your spouse on a bad day?) Instead we always greet each other at the door with a kiss hello, share what the other could do to help (as in "I could really use your big warm arms around me right now"), dress up for each other, have special date nights, send passionate cards, notes, and e-mails expressing gratitude, and complimenting each other as much as possible. (Even if it's just "thanks for getting the toilet paper" or "thanks for listening to me babble about my boss the jerk.") The goal is to keep loving, appreciating, and forgiving your spouse the way you want to be loved, appreciated, and forgiven.

16

LIABILITIES OF THE
LOVE BUSINESS

You would expect that fixing up someone with the perfect spouse would ensure a lifelong friendship, right? Well, unfortunately that's not always the case. My matchmaker and I are no longer in touch, and I've fallen out with several of the couples I've combined over the years. I've found that playing romantic roulette can be dangerous and risky, for many reasons.

Although introducing singles seems like a fun, easy, and amusing activity, there is a serious, dark, and intrusive side to the practice. Setting up someone romantically means in a sense that you are getting into his bedroom and choosing whom he should sleep with. You might be seeing him at his most needy, sad, and vulnerable. Although your motives may be beautiful and pure, you can never control what will happen when you put two single souls together. Hell, they don't even know what the outcome will be. All kinds of emotions, ego dramas, entanglements, and chain reactions can crop up out of nowhere, and you don't want to get caught in the middle of the cross fire. So before giving out your friend's phone number, planning a double date with a close relative, or throwing a swinging singles party, be aware of the ways this very complex, intimate connection can completely backfire on you.

Typecasting: Singles sometimes have quirky, unrealistic images of themselves. They could be horrified, enraged, or offended by the age, looks, status, smarts, or lack of smarts they perceive in the match you set them up with. Rita, a forty-three-year-old unattached writer friend, once called me, shrieking that the handsome forty-five-year-old lawyer I'd fixed her up with was completely classless and stupid, and she was offended that I had no idea who she was at all. (He just married a beautiful thirty-three-year-old DA, and I know that Rita's still broke, highbrow, and single.) Lois, a sixty-eight-year-old professor I met through a fellow writer, felt hurt when I introduced her to a seventy-nine-year-old "ancient old man," as if I were insulting her. Truth be told, they looked the same age. (Lois is still living alone, while he soon married someone less judgmental.) Still, people are very sensitive and vain when it comes to their looks, age, and status. So you should first ask singles whom they see themselves with and what their parameters for partners are. If you sense a disconnect between reality and fantasy, tread carefully. Or sidestep fix-ups completely.

Dr. Jekyll and Mr. Hyde Monsters: Some solo men and women appear perfectly normal and sane during the course of your friendship. Yet there's something about sex or courtship that brings out their mean, bizarre, or sick side. Aaron's divorced comedy-writing colleague Rudy, who was always pleasant and amiable around us, turned out to be creepy when it came to dating. He wined and dined my friend Debbie. Then, the minute after he slept with her, he said he had no interest in dating her, though he would have sex with her again. On a first date with my close ally Stephanie, he confided to her that he'd screwed around on his ex-wife for almost their entire marriage. (Did he think this would impress Stephanie? Or that she wouldn't tell me about what Rudy did to his ex, whom I knew?) Since he was Aaron's good friend, I still didn't want to believe he was a bad guy. Plus I always guessed that a fix-up's feedback could be one-sided, mistaken, with quotes repeated out of context. So I gave him one more shot. On a casual double dinner date with my friend Dara, Rudy blatantly ignored her during the meal. When the check came, he counted out exact change, making it clear that he was not going to treat for her, then ran into a cab the second we got outside. Diagnosis: while Rudy was a fun buddy to Aaron, with females he was a raving misogynist. I called all three women to apologize. (They were pleased I'd confirmed their negative feelings about him.) I crossed Rudy off all of my lists and never invited him anywhere again. I also try not to be shocked now when someone reveals he is not as classy and together as he first appeared. You never really know what someone is like with the opposite sex. Don't make too many assumptions based on a casual friendship.

Bitter Breakups: If you put a pair together and they fall madly in love, but ultimately it doesn't work out, you could be taken to task by one or both parties. With the two couples I set up who have parted, neither of the men have spoken to me. It could be they are afraid I'll blame them. Or they blame me. Either way, almost 50 percent of marriages in this country don't last. So be prepared for parting sorrow and don't blame yourself. People sometimes need to point the finger at someone else to avoid facing their own failures, disappointments, and inadequacies. On the other hand, consider the potential damage before fixing up anyone flip-pantly. Be especially careful if you're setting up your boss, business partner, or someone you'll need to work with again on a regular basis. I sometimes discuss the ending in advance and make a potential match promise that no matter what happens, she'll end it amiably.

Hidden Jealousy: Even when you are blissfully married, if you set up a duo that has a wedding reception more lavish than yours, or takes a six-month honeymoon around the world, or buys a bigger condo, or becomes rich and famous, it can cause all kinds of unexpected envy to surface. This hit home when I was going through infertility while my sister-in-law Monica was giving birth to each of her four children. Though I was very happy for her, I resented how they soon took over all family dinners, holidays, and vacations. I don't regret the fix-up at all, but I did need a few extra therapy sessions to come to terms with my own "biological tragedy." I also adjusted my travel schedule so I could avoid big events with all the kids. Instead I try to hang out with my nieces and nephews one-on-one and see my parents alone so I don't feel pushed out of my own family tree.

The Role of Referee: While it's fun to fix up a couple that hits it off, sometimes both sides of your match will expect you to mediate their issues and fights. You have to walk a fine line between trying to be helpful and not putting your foot in your mouth. When Jasmine asked my advice about her husband, Daniel, who she complained was lazy and watched too much television, I told her to find friends of her own and leave him alone. He was eighty years old and retired, after all. She was unusually active and young for sixty-five. And if watching TV was a fair cause for divorce, most couples in this country would be kaput. She went ahead and left him, which strained our relationship. I have since learned to keep my opinions to myself and say, "Oh it's call waiting, gotta go," to keep myself out of other people's love trouble.

Wedding Extravaganzas: Friends and family members often expect their matchmaker to attend their engagement party, bridal shower, rehearsal dinner, wedding reception, Sunday brunch, baby shower, birth at the hospital, bris, or baby-naming ceremony, sometimes acting as if attendance is mandatory, along with bringing an appropriate present for each function. Then there's every subsequent anniversary party and birthday soiree for each of their children. One matchmaker I know refused to buy any gifts, saying she already "gave at the office" by introducing the happy couple. You must set limits and learn to say, "Sorry, I can't make it," without feeling guilty. After all, you did already give them your all, and there would not be any of these celebrations if not for you.

Unrealistic Expectations: Once you've fixed up a marriage, other relatives and friends of the bride will approach you, tell you their type, and insist on being set up too. Word gets around and people say, "Oh, Sue's a great fixer-upper. Sue, you have to fix up Aunt Jane." This is sometimes said with the sixty-four-year-old, three-times divorced, alcoholic Aunt Jane standing right there, enthusiastically telling me how she prefers athletic men in their forties. It's hard to explain that I only offer my free services to pals when the mood hits. And not when I'm faced with a needy stranger whose feelings I don't want to hurt.

Overinvestment: When I get a love vibe about a potential long-term pair, I feel excited about all the promise. Especially when a best buddy of mine sparks to a good pal of Aaron's. Sometimes I get too gung ho, especially if one or both of the couple e-mails and calls me with the latest up-dates, asks advice, and tells all our mutual friends what an amazing fixer-upper I am. Instead of getting my own work done, I start daydreaming, imagining double dates, joint vacations, and helping plan the wedding reception. I've learned to keep my distance, not talk too much about early relationship stages, not ask questions or follow up, and let people I've set up come to me. There's nothing wrong with a little vicarious thrill. Unless it doesn't work out, and my heart gets a little broken too.

17

HOW TO KEEP FIXING UP
YOURSELF AND YOUR MATE

Obviously the off-Broadway play title *I Love You, You're Perfect, Now Change* implies that altering someone to your specifications is bad, and Billy Joel's song "I Love You Just the Way You Are" is supposed to be good. Yet Joel wrote those lyrics about the wife he wound up dumping for a blond supermodel (who later dumped him back). A more realistic route to everlasting love is to trade instant chemistry and starstruck illusions for the bare bones of a good brain, heart, and soul connection. Then be willing to do a lot of work and compromise—on your partner, yourself, and your relationship. Of course, your timing and manner will determine the results.

Good communication between couples is essential to any decent connection. After you've been dating for a year, it's normal for your romance to get more realistic. If you are living together, engaged, pregnant, seriously considering marriage, or even already wed, you should not fear bringing up difficult subjects. That's especially true if potential deal breakers are your partner's smoking, drinking, swearing, gambling, shopaholic tendencies, workaholism, travel schedule, sloppy grooming habits, big weight gain, eating disorder, intrusive family members, or obnoxious best friend.

If there were a hidden reason that your lover was pulling away from you, wouldn't you want to know exactly what it was? Instead of your fear that he's having an affair, or might not really still feel attracted to you, maybe he just can't stand that you don't shave your legs often enough. Or perhaps she does enjoy sex with you—just not when you reek of cigarette smoke. Yes, it might initially hurt your feelings to hear what's really been going on inside your partner's head. But if one tic or imperfection was causing your potential spouse to pull away, wouldn't you want the chance to change it? Sometimes telling the truth can lead to productive trade-offs and transformations. When my husband urged me to quit my twenty-seven-year two-pack-a-day cigarette habit, I then felt justified in pushing him to lose his junk-food fetish and lose weight. I've been smoke-free for five years now. He's seventy pounds thinner than when we married. So we're both healthier, cleaner, and better off, as is our relationship.

How to Change Something about Your Partner

Try Honey, Not Vinegar: If you want your partner to quit a horrible habit, work on improving certain skills, or amend something else about himself, never, ever begin the conversation with negativity, superiority, or any kind of insult. Instead, always start conversations with caring gestures and sweet compliments. "Honey, you are really so gorgeous, smart, kind, and adorable. I know this is silly and superficial of me, but when you leave clothes on the floor, it makes me crazy."

Use Self-Deprecation: Poking fun at yourself can poke holes in the tension. If you're a neatnik, say things like, "I realize I'm being a bit anal and picky here," or use specific aspects of your past to analyze where your neatness comes from. For example, start by saying, "You know as one of six kids in a big messy house, it means so much to me to live in a nice clean environment now."

Know and Admit Your Issues First: Having been the eldest child with three smart younger male siblings, I was interrupted often and constantly felt usurped of attention and praise. So I am particularly sensitive to being undermined and ignored. If my husband cuts me off or hogs the conversation (as most type-A people do), I do not yell, "Stop interrupting me! You are being rude and hogging the floor!" Instead I say, "Honey, I have problems from my past with feeling overshadowed by males. When you only keep talking about the TV show you're working on, I feel invisible, like I'm a failure. If you'd ask about me and my work, I'd feel much better." Instead of alienating someone, it makes him like, relate to, and understand how to help and please you.

Consider a Compromise: My husband hates going to crowded parties and other big events. I adore them. That's why we came up with the rule that I can go to any social function I want, for as long as I want. But—unless it's dinner with my boss or the wedding of a close relative of mine—he does not have to attend. This way we both get what we want.

Offer an Alternative: I did not just let my husband know that I wasn't crazy about many ripped, old items of clothing in his closet. I slowly replaced them with beautiful new items instead. This started after just three months of dating, when I hated to see him lying around in his torn jeans and ripped T-shirt. So I bought him a beautiful black Italian robe as a present. Every time he wore it, I told him how handsome he looked and ran my fingers over its soft threads. Maybe that's why he still wears it!

Try Positive Reinforcement: Instead of saying, "You look like a grizzly bum when you don't shave for three days," I waited until my husband did shave. Then I ran my hands over his face, kissed him, and said, "You look so handsome when you're clean cut." This usually got him back to the razor regularly. Similarly, instead of telling me, "I hate how dumpy you look in those baggy old jeans and big T-shirts," he began buying me sexy outfits. Whenever I would wear them, he'd put his arms around me and say, "You look so gorgeous in that dress," which made me want to dress up for him more.

It Goes Both Ways: The minute you start dissecting your love's diet and exercise regime, hair and grooming customs, spending methods, or smoking/drinking/partying routines, she has the right to scrutinize your style, habits, and compulsions in return. If you think you are perfect and don't have anything more to work on, you're fooling yourself. Acknowledge your faults and limitations, and realize that the more willing you are to change to please your spouse, the more willing she will probably be to please you.

Offer a Specific Trade-Off: Although my husband was very busy juggling three jobs at the same time last summer, I really wanted his comments on the rough draft of a new book I was working on. Instead of just asking him outright, I made him an offer he couldn't refuse: I would let him out of a bunch of social events he hated, along with our Saturday-evening date nights, if instead of attending he would read a few chapters and make notes for me. We tried it for six weeks. He got his work done and I got his feedback on my project. I made sure to thank him and show gratitude. (Plus the promise that if it sold for a fortune I would pay off our mortgage.)

Your choice of bargaining chips can even be kooky and not comparable. Last week we argued about two issues—Aaron wanted to get his hair cut short, while I love it long. Then his sister offered him their old childhood pinball machine, which he wanted to keep at our place. I didn't think we had room. I wound up offering to try the pinball machine in the corner, if he'd leave his long curls alone, and he agreed. The trick is to both win something you want, whatever the swap.

When in Doubt, Get a Mediator: If what you want is serious and heavy, as in confronting your spouse about quitting drinking, drugs, having affairs, or other destructive behavior, ask a neutral member of the family, clergy, or a couples therapist to intervene before you end it all or make things worse. My girlfriend Debbie's husband, Pete, took drugs and drove their daughter to school stoned. In Debbie's view, their relationship was over. But an experienced marriage counselor did crisis intervention, sent him right to rehab, then made Pete sign a contract, swearing he would never take drugs again. That was six years ago. He's been clean, vigilant, and repentant the entire time and their family is now thriving.

Save It for Later: No matter how much you wish your husband or wife was thinner, buffer, better dressed or coiffed, less impatient, kinder to you, or hotter, you must watch your timing and his feelings. Right after he was fired from his job, an hour before Christmas dinner, or on the way to a wedding or a funeral is usually not the time to share your desire for your spouse to improve. It might make him feel angry, self-conscious, or hurt, and want to cancel. If this issue has been bothering you for nine years, okay, go for it. But if your spouse just got a haircut, new clothes, and glasses last week, like you asked, give your latest renovation fantasy a rest or go back to Chapter 2 and keep fixing yourself up. Remember that you pledged to be with this person for richer, poorer, in sickness, and in health, forever, and vice versa. You are very lucky to be out of the cold and complicated dating and mating scene and safe inside with someone warm whom you love. Try your criticism, perfectionism, complaints, and kvetches when it will be best received. The beauty of marriage is that you can resume bugging the hell out of your mate again tomorrow.

Save the Ultimatums for Life-and-Death Issues: Driving drunk or high, or otherwise compromising your spouse's or children's safety, is nonnegotiable. So is gambling away all of your savings in Las Vegas, lying, cheating, doing crystal meth, and any kind of physical, emotional, or verbal abuse. For all other complaints, get some perspective before threatening to leave and risking your love's feelings.

Don't Get Defensive: Having an open conversation about what bothers you and your partner about each other can be scary and painful. Try not to respond quickly to anything that makes you angry or uncomfortable. Sometimes I find taking a walk alone for a break helps. So does taking notes, or responding by e-mail, phone, or letter the next day. Don't blurt out a mean, sarcastic, or definitive response right away that you could regret.

Pick Your Battles Carefully: I liked that the relationship books *He's Just Not That Into You* and *The Rules* reinforced the need for women to have strong self-esteem and high expectations about how they should be treated. Yet some women take that to mean their spouses should be buying them special gifts for their birthday, anniversary, and

Valentine's Day, and get offended and hurt if they don't. In my experience, the husband who offers his wife jewelry, flowers, chocolate, perfume, and plane tickets to Paris can be found more often on celluloid than in reality.

In more than a decade together, my fabulous husband bought me an expensive, romantic gift once: my engagement ring. In the last ten years, he has never brought home another piece of jewelry, or given me another big-deal present—unless I picked it out myself, then reminded, begged, or threatened him at least three times. He doesn't like cards, has forgotten holidays, and lets me know that he thinks Valentine's Day is stupid. I have chosen to let this go. Instead, I focus on his positive traits, generosity, and what he does give me. I love my ring and my mate who—after all—married me, critiqued my latest project, came to many literary events for my two memoirs even though he hated being written about, helped me overcome major addictions, and let me make a real estate deal with all of our money, not to mention control every aspect of the three-month renovation he would rather have avoided. I feel extremely well loved and protected, if not showered in thoughtful cards and presents. He is that into me, he's just not that into shopping.

My father is not known for surprising my mother with diamonds, furs, or flowers either. On the other hand, for fifty-two years he has been a hardworking, devoted, and faithful husband, father to her four children, and now he's a sweet grandfather to five grandkids. What our husbands give us is more important than overpriced roses that will die in three days or gold adornments. My mother and I thank our lucky stars every day and buy ourselves—or each other—perfume, flowers, candy, jewelry, and plane tickets.

Don't Insist That Your Point of View Is Correct: Even if you have an important side that needs to be expressed and heard, rigidity is rarely the way to negotiate anything. You never want to rub in how smart, sane, or correct you are, since that could hurt, undermine, emasculate, or insult your partner. It's so much nicer to be in love with the warm (albeit imperfect) person beside you than to be very right and very alone.

18

HOW TO BECOME A FIX-UP FANATIC TOO

If you think your single friend, parent, sibling, cousin, schoolmate, accountant, boss, colleague, or neighbor might be interested in meeting someone you have in mind, here are some simple steps to becoming a great matchmaker.

Ask First: Make sure the person you want to set up is open, available, and in the mood to meet somebody. Maybe she is not ready, or is quietly seeing somebody already that you don't know about. Inquire what kind of person she might want to meet and listen carefully to the answer.

Plan a Little Get-Together: It could be breakfast, luncheon, dinner, drinks, dancing, local literary reading, charity event, Academy Awards party, or Super Bowl bash. The trick is to invite mostly solo players. It doesn't have to be lavish or expensive. If your home is geographically out of the way or not big enough, have everybody meet in the back room of a local restaurant, bar, or club you belong to.

Even getting a table at Starbucks or the coffee bar at Barnes & Noble can create new connections if you pick good people and introduce everyone well.

Holiday Hostess: You can easily include several extra unattached guests at your Thanksgiving meal, Christmas lunch, Hanukkah dinner, Valentine's Day soiree, St. Patrick's Day celebration, or Halloween costume party. Sometimes themes and rituals help break the ice—like green beer, singing carols together, playing dreidel, or well-placed mistletoe. But don't invite only one solo male and female and the rest couples and kids. That will make it too obvious that it's a setup. Plus one cancellation and you've planned the night from hell for anyone single.

Keep a Few Couples Around: I have learned that having an event with all singles, on the other hand, can be too conspicuous and make people feel self-consciously on display. Feng shui suggests using double objects, like turtle doves, for decoration; I like to place a few happy human couples around the party for good love karma. Even though Aaron dislikes social events, I sometimes beg him to make a late appearance, and friends have let me know that they found his sweeping kiss hello to me sweet and inspiring. (Even if he then hides the rest of the night in his den, aka The Bat Cave.) Having Dina and Ted, the adorable newlyweds I set up, at a recent singles party added a success story and romantic energy to the whole room.

Be Low-Key: Being casual, easygoing, and comfortable is usually the way to go when it comes to clothes, decor, food, and invitations (in person, by phone, or by e-mail will do). There's something about dress codes, seating arrangements, and sit-down dinners that makes people uptight and rigid. Most guests are much more fun and calm while sitting on the couch and sharing a beer and eating fried chicken with their fingers.

Any Setting Can Be Romantic: Just dim the lights, light candles, play sexy music (Marvin Gaye, Al Green, Nora Jones, or Macy Gray come to mind), serve light food, keep wine or champagne flowing, take pictures, or have a poster or book for guests to sign. One friend puts huge rolls of paper around her walls and leaves out crayons, asking everyone to draw a self-portrait. When people are nervous, it's easier to have props and things to drink, draw, eat, and do.

Be Creative with the Guest List: Don't invite the same old crowd where everybody already knows each other. Call some of your exes (if they're single), locate old classmates you haven't seen in a while, and extend yourself to coworkers or neighbors you think might be nice or interesting. Mix ages, backgrounds, and professions whenever possible. If you have the room and inclination, ask all your guests to bring a single pal with them.

Take a Chance on Someone Who Seems Lonely: As someone who had no real friends until third grade, I still fondly recall the few other kids in elementary school who were nice to me and invited me to their birthday parties. So now I try to reciprocate, pick up stray singles who might need a new friend, and invite them to join in. These loners are usually sweeter and more appreciative than those in the sought-after popular crowd. Stewart, a divorced colleague in his fifties from out of the country, was so appreciative to be invited to a party at my home that he sent me a gorgeous bouquet of flowers that morning. Then he showed up with a very fancy bottle of Scotch. Even better, he clicked with my cousin Michelle, took her out to a beautiful dinner, and they remain e-mail and pen pals!

Help with Mingling: Don't just introduce people who don't know each other by saying their names. It's much more helpful if you can relay amusing or interesting facts about them, their job, or their hobbies. For example, saying, "My friend Dagmar, who is from Prague, is a corporate lawyer who loves literary readings" gave interested men many openings: one commented on a recent trip he took to Prague, another lawyer sparked to her legal profession. A journalist mentioned a book he'd recently enjoyed and asked if she'd read it, and then wound up asking her out. If you are terrible at remembering names or don't know enough details about your guests, you might want to consider name tags and asking a few friends or cohosts to assist you with the introducing duties.

Trust Your Fix-Up Instincts: You've probably already successfully put people together before, for different reasons. Many friends recommend their doctor, contractor, architect, real estate agent, lawyer, or accountant to other friends. Setting up romance starts with the same nice helpful impulse. Someone you like has a need or a void that she wants to fill. If you like someone and think she is a good person, you assume your pal might feel the same way. Although ages, looks, class, careers, background, and interests could be taken into account, you don't have to analyze or overthink all the complicated elements before acting. Throwing together several single friends at a party or holiday dinner is a great way to test the waters, see how it feels, and take a chance.

Keep Expectations Low: Don't set yourself up to fail by thinking everyone has to show up for it to be a great party. Many people who RSVP yes will wind up skipping out, without reason. Something as dumb as rain, a little snow, or a heat wave can also scare guests off. Assume there will be some no-shows and don't sweat it. Don't tell anyone, "You are going to meet the love of your life tonight, I can just feel it," or, "I know this is the person you are going to marry." Just tell everyone the plan is to meet some nice new friends. Don't focus on or even mention people who said they'd come but don't. It's their loss. Instead lavish attention and praise on the guests who do show.

Prepare to Dazzle: Whenever possible, I plan a party or evening event in advance on a quiet day, when I have little work to do. That way I can get my hair done, get a manicure or pedicure, shop for party stuff, go to the gym, or get a massage. I like to have a few hours alone beforehand, so I can put out the food, prepare, and carefully set up while dancing around to James Brown. I also like to wear good-luck charms, or a bunch of silver bracelets that clang when I move quickly. Thus I'm more charming, sparkling, and filled with good calm karma by the time my guests arrive. The host's mood and attitude set the tone for any event.

It's About Sharing: Being warm, kind, generous, and giving can be contagious. So thank your guests for coming, and immediately compliment them on anything you like about them—whether it's a new sweater, a haircut, or a smile. Having too much food and drink is better than running out. Everybody loves goody bags, even if they just contain candy, stickers, or trinkets. I once bought ten rolls of instant Polaroid film and let each guest take home a picture of himself. I also offer extra bottles of wine or doggy bags of the leftover food to anybody who helped me out, any students I know to be broke, or the last guests to leave. (That way I don't eat everything myself while cleaning up at three in the morning.) I write down and try to remember to show gratitude to anybody who brought me a bottle of wine, flowers, or desserts. My former student Stacey brought a big box of cream puffs to my last party. At the end of the evening, the guest of honor left with her entourage, then slipped back inside to grab three more cream puffs and stuff them into her mouth when she thought nobody was looking. I e-mailed the anecdote to Stacey, who told me I'd made her day. And I bet she brings more cream puffs my way!

Make Follow-Up Easy: Bring cards or fliers, or at least have pen and paper handy. I often hand out my business card, which has my phone number on it. I also give out postcards for my latest reading, book event, or seminar, which includes my e-mail. This works wonders for people who are too shy to ask for each other's info and would prefer to get it through me. I always ask first before I give out anybody else's info, which serves as a screening process.

Let People Be Mysterious and Cryptic: Most singles who are ready to meet that special someone let their matchmaker know whom they like and don't like. Since I'm blunt, literal minded, and goal oriented, I prefer straight shooters who respond this way. Yet I recently introduced six interesting, unattached colleagues at a party who either hadn't yet decided who liked whom, or didn't want to share it with me. When I asked a woman in the mix who she'd date, she just said, "All three guys are nice." When I asked one of the guys if he'd sparked to any specific gal there, he said, "Dating is like poker and I don't want to show my hand yet." Although I don't see love as anything like a card game, I held my tongue and realized that everybody is entitled to have a different romantic style. Meanwhile they all went on two group outings, everyone said it was fun, and who knows? I may get to add another notch to my matchmaking belt yet.

Be Discreet: If you want to later schmooze about who liked whom and who asked for whose phone numbers, limit it to your spouse, friends, matchmaker, or party coplanner. Keep negative gossip—like who got drunk and who wound up sleeping with whom—as harmless and nameless as possible. On the other hand, sometimes if someone liked someone it's cute to share the enthusiasm. When Aaron's colleague Jeff met my friend Peggy as he was leaving our place, he went home and e-mailed me three words: "She's a goddess," a message I of course forwarded to Peggy.

How Not to Be a Fix-Up Fanatic

Don't Force Your Fix-Ups on Anyone: No means no. It doesn't mean invite your single girlfriend to Christmas dinner to surprise your brother, despite the fact that he already told you, "No way, José." There are very good reasons why single people say no or not now when you offer to introduce them. Respect their wishes. There are plenty of unattached humans dying to find partners who will say yes immediately, mean it, and greatly appreciate your efforts. Never be intrusive or force your services on anybody who's not interested.

Don't Try to Control Who Should Be with Whom: Just because you have decided Paul is clean cut and adorable and your kid cousin should marry him doesn't mean she won't prefer the plumber with tattoos and nose rings. Leave room for personal style, individual tastes, and idiosyncratic preferences. That's why inviting groups of people to parties and events sometimes works better than one-on-one setups. Do not make assumptions that your cousin's or friend's taste will mirror your own. If interest in a certain someone is revealed, do not criticize, especially if your take is based on superficial qualities.

Do Not Lie: I know you want to build up your friend Daria so Dan goes nuts for her. But if you say she's skinny and gorgeous, when she shows up looking like Roseanne, he is going to notice. Likewise, if Kevin is unemployed, don't tell his potential soul mate, Eric, otherwise. If you know that Lester has only just separated from his wife, do not describe him as divorced. Remember, you are hooking up a person you care about with somebody she could invite into her home, bed, family, and inner circle. A good match-maker will never start or perpetuate any kind of falsehoods. Any lies you tell could haunt you—and your single friend— in the future.

Don't Make People Pay: I try to invite guests I don't know to my house or to free readings and parties that won't cost them anything except for their own transportation. If you have a gathering at a restaurant or tavern, warn everyone in advance whether it's a cash bar or that dinners could run each person a hundred dollars. If it's a charity auction or art show, make it clear how much tickets will cost and how you expect to be paid. Not everybody carries enough cash or a credit card, and some people cannot afford to pay. As a broke freelance writer, there was nothing worse than sur-prise costs I couldn't afford cropping up in the middle of the evening. Know the financial status of your crowd and be conscious of gifts one is expected to bring, donations to be made, parking costs, and taxi rides home. Making some-one feel ashamed or embarrassed socially could ruin his night, his potential date's night, and yours too.

Don't Put Pressure on Potential Pairs: "You're going to meet your husband tonight," or, "My friend Lisa is so amazing I'm sure you two will totally hit it off," is not usu-ally a good way to go. It sets up very high expectations that could make everyone uncomfortable if the two designated daters don't hit it off, or prefer somebody else at the party. "Dave is one of my favorite people in the world. Let me introduce you," or, "I'd love you to meet my friend Lisa," is as strong as the wording should get.

Don't Let Your Issues and Prejudices Come into Play: Even if you are married to a tall, Jewish, Boston businessman with Ivy League pedigree and dark, curly hair, there's nothing wrong with your fellow Jewish girlfriend hooking up with somebody Muslim, Protestant, Catholic, black, Latino, Asian or short, fat, thin, or bald who lives in the Bronx and writes poetry or paints scenery at the local theater. The only relevant questions are "Is he kind?" or "Does she make you happy?"

Don't Follow Up Too Fast or Furiously: If people are interested and want to see each other again, they will contact you. Putting somebody on the spot twelve hours after the rendezvous with, "So, what did you think of my friend? Are you going to call her again or what?" is way too pushy. If you are dying to know if the date took place and how it went, try an innocuous e-mail, such as "How's everything going? Did you have a nice weekend?"

Don't Take Sides: If one person had an argument with someone at your event, or if after a few dates somebody feels slighted, you can be sympathetic. But try not to jump in there and decide who is at fault. You weren't there. People can be neurotic and extremely inaccurate when recapping conversations and any kind of carnal activity. There are often three sides to every story—his, hers, and the right one. You can say, "I'm so sorry your feelings were hurt." But if at all possible, try to stay neutral.

Don't Get Too Involved: This is not your relationship. If your male coworker didn't treat your sister for dinner, that wasn't so generous of him. But it's their problem, not yours.

You can be sympathetic or give her advice if she asks. But do not call to yell at him. If your best friend Caren ran out of the café after drinks, bailing on dinner with your accountant, Steven, that sucks, but it's not your fault. Once you introduce people, you cannot control them and you are not responsible for their actions.

Don't Be a Sarcastic, Loose-Lipped Gossipmonger: A person looking for a life partner can be very vulnerable and scared. Putting people together well is an art that often requires silence, grace, compassion, and discretion. It is an honor to have somebody confide her deepest hopes and fears to you. Treat the information she tells you the way you would want your secrets handled. Remember that every mistake you make could come back to bite you.

Don't Say Yes When You Mean No: If someone you've invited over asks if they can bring their single pals who you've never met, do not feel obligated to comply if you don't feel like it. "Sorry, it's an invitation-only soiree" is a perfectly acceptable response. I learned that more isn't always the merrier the hard way, when my close confidant Shoshana asked if she could bring a new buddy along to a bash I was throwing. I'd spent a long time finding several special fortyish single men I wanted a few special fortyish girlfriends of mine to meet. But I dumbly told Shoshana it was okay. The added woman I'd reluctantly agreed to let in turned out to be twenty-two, floozier and more liquor-loving than the important guests I'd invited. The miniskirted flirt wound up getting drunk and making out with the forty-four-year-old surgeon bachelor I'd wanted Shoshana—or one of my other close friends—to meet. So being unnecessarily accommodating actually marred my and Shoshana's night.

Don't Be Impatient: Romance can be a rocky road, and those on the journey often need to take two steps forward, one step back. I know you wish your child, sibling, boss, employee, or best friend would hurry the hell up, get over his stupid loser ex-lover, marry the fabulous fix-up you introduced him to, and invite you to his wedding already. But if he breaks up with his sweet new gal to jump back into the sack with Ms. Wrong, don't be shocked, freak out, or lash out. There are many complex motivations at work, perhaps including fear of intimacy, repeating old family patterns, or self-hatred. It took me many years to work out my relationship issues—and my parents lived the American Dream, are still happy together, and adored me. Be as patient, sympathetic, and compassionate as humanly possible. Before saying something you might regret, hold your tongue and remember what you were like in your worst stage of love confusion. It's rarely helpful to say, "You're being an idiot," "Your ex-lover is being an idiot," or "I told you so."

Don't Go It Alone: Fixing up people is much more fun when you have a partner in crime. When Aaron admitted that a few of his available pals wanted to be on my love list, I placed them on top priority. After his friend John took out my comrade Sally five times, Aaron asked, "Have they slept together yet?" He was clearly sharing the vicarious thrills of matchmaking with me. If, once in a while, he still berates me for being a busybody, I remind him of our first rendezvous. That was when he first looked at me and said, "Valerie was right. You are beautiful," a line I suggest all nice single guys use at least once, preferably on one of my single girlfriends.

Acknowledgments

I would like to express my deepest gratitude to . . .

- My "core pillars" CR, Elizabeth Kaplan, Danielle Perez, and Fred Woolverton for their brilliance, loyalty, and devotion.

- My NYC dream team Barb Burg, Rachael Dorman, Susan Corcoran, Patricia Ballantyne, Shannon Jamieson Vazquez, Matthew Martin, Margaret Kopp, and Webmaster Eric Shapiro for their insight, invaluable help, and patience.

- Editors Julie Just, Clare Lambe, Esther Haynes, Elizabeth Shaw, Chrissy Persico, Michael Molyneux, Frank Flaherty, Christopher Moore, Faye Penn, Emma Segal, Ruth Andrew Ellenson, Laurie Muchnick, Margo Hammond, Ryan Harbage, Harvey Shapiro, and Devan Sipher for their support and wisdom.

- Laurel Touby, Taffy Akner, Erwin Ong, Alison Mitchell, Donna Rauch, Mike Debroyn, Carla Oliver,

Daryl Mattson, Lita Weissman, Linda Friedman, Amy Stanton, Keith Hewitt, Ellen Cavolino, Felicia Sullivan, Sarah McNally, Lee Hilton, Mike Schwartz, Teri Morof, Lisa Applebaum, and Karen Sosnick for the coolest book events on the planet.

- My colleagues Robert Polito, Deborah Landau, Jackson Taylor, Laura Cronk, Luis Jarmillo, Carmen Scheidel, Elizabeth Maxwell, Bob Blaisdell, and Ian Frazier for letting me teach the "instant gratification takes too long" method of journalism.

- Photographer Danny Brownstein, the Kahns, Bobby Bepary and his crew at University Copy, George Margetousakis and the Cozy's gang for their TLC and compassion at all hours.

- Writers Ronit Pinto, Tory Connolly Walker, Sheila Callahan, Lynn Harris, Rachel Kramer Bussel, Melissa Whitworth, Carolyn Nardiello, Lois Brady Smith, Matthew Flamm, Seth Kugel, Krysten Weller, Lucia Poster, Jake Cooney, John Mangarella, Chris Pacetta, Idra Rosenberg, Lynne Schreiber, Sherry Amatenstein, Cindy Frenkel, Michael Freidson, Karine Cohen, Laura Silver, Marci Alboher, and Rima Suqi for their beautiful articles, which I still shlep around with me in my briefcase.

- Friends and mentors Kristin Kemp, Kate Walter, Tony Powell, Alice Phillips, Wendy Shanker, Nicole Bokat, Stacey Kramer, Diane Schwabble, Rob Bates, Jerry Portwood, Rafique Kathwari, Jill Hamburg-Coplan, Roberta Bernstein, Liza Monroy, Harold James, Amy Hill, Stan Mieses, Susan Jane Gilman, Rich Prior, Jessica Seigel, Karen Salmansohn, Gerry Jonas, Isadore Century, Roz Lacks, Doris Vallejo, Alan Kinsberg, Larry Bergreen, Laura Berman, Ruth

Gruber, and Molly Jong-Fast for their astute criticism, kindness, and eternal encouragement.

- Close confidants Judy Burdick, Arlene Cohen, Dagmar Schwartz, Mimi Fast, Serena Richard, Lisa Rosenthal, Rina Drucker, Lucille Rubin, Ivy Landsman, Stacey Greenwald, Andrea Miller, Gary Kordan, and Gary Rubin for saying "call when you get weird" and always picking up the phone.

- My L.A. family Jane Wald, Kathryn Glasgow, Jody Podolsky, Caren Emmer, Lori Monheim, Sally Helfer, Amy Alkon, Timmy, Shawn Goodman, Anita Rosenberg, Alison Powell, and Amy Klein for driving me around and choosing my reading over the Golden Globes.

- To my warm and funny Midwest family, for flying to New York for my book party and for all their love and honesty, even when screaming "Stop writing about me!"